LOW-SALT
DASH DINNERS

SANDRA NOWLAN

FORMAC PUBLISHING COMPANY LIMITED
HALIFAX

This book is dedicated to my bright and lively grandchildren: Kieran and Cameron Calder and Eva, Adah and Abigail Hatfield who love to get in the kitchen and cook up their own magic.

PHOTO CREDITS

Cover photography: Jen Partridge.
All interior photos by Jen Partridge, except where noted below:
iStock: 15, 23, 33, 36, 48, 71, 72, 76, 77, 81, 90, 100, 110, 115, 124, 128, 134, 135, 136, 141, 147, 149; Meghan Collins: 19, 43, 86, 120, 125, 142, 145, 150; Timeless Gourmet: 99.

Formac Publishing Company Limited recognizes the support of the Province of Nova Scotia through the Department of Canadian Tourism, Culture and Heritage. We acknowledge the financial support of the Government of Canada through the Canada Book Fund for our publishing activities.

NOVA SCOTIA
Tourism, Culture and Heritage

Canadä

Library and Archives Canada Cataloguing in Publication

Nowlan, Sandra
    Low-salt DASH dinners / Sandra Nowlan.

Includes index.
Issued also in an electronic format.
ISBN 978-0-88780-940-8

    1. Hypertension—Diet therapy—Recipes. 2. Salt-free diet—Recipes. 3. Quick and easy cookery. I. Title.

RC685.H8N72 2010   641.5'6323   C2010-902647-0

Formac Publishing Company Limited
5502 Atlantic Street
Halifax, Nova Scotia
B3H 1G4
www.formac.ca

Printed and bound in China

CONTENTS

INTRODUCTION

A diagnosis of hypertension can be devastating when the physician prescribes a low-salt diet. The initial thought often is: I am doomed to a bland diet and can't have my favourite foods anymore. If you had a diet heavy in processed food, or fast food high in sodium, you will be in for a change, but most people can modify their recipes and cooking techniques to produce a tasty and varied diet. The enjoyment of good food is one of the great pleasures of life and, with a little ingenuity, delicious food can be prepared without depending on salt for flavour.

This book is designed to give you lots of ideas for simple low-salt dinners that are delicious, easy-to-prepare and suitable for everyday meals. The recipes have an interesting flair and a variety of intriguing tastes that will make low-salt and low-fat food appealing.

This book is a sequel to my first low-salt cookbook, *Delicious DASH Flavours,* which had a positive reception across Canada. Both books follow the guidelines of the DASH (Dietary Approaches to Stop Hypertension) eating plan but differ in their focus. Recipes in the first book are mainly from top Canadian chefs and offer a wide variety of specialty dishes, many suitable for special occasions. The theme of this book is simpler recipes for everyday dinners using readily available ingredients.

Most of these recipes come from my collection of family favourites. They have evolved over the years as I am always looking for ways to make them more interesting and delicious. They include exceptional recipes from friends, and a variety of different ethnic dishes. The challenge was to see if they were still tasty after removing salt and reducing fat. Additional recipes have been selected from Canadian chefs.

I had a number of criteria in selecting recipes. The key consideration was great flavour and texture. Fresh ingredients played a major role in assuring top-notch quality. The dishes had to be colourful and interesting and have an element of fun in preparation and/or presentation. Ingredients had to be easy to find at a reasonable price. Imagination and innovation came into play in replacing salt with seasonings, and in selecting garnishes. Of course, the food had to be nutritious and in accordance with the DASH guidelines.

We tested over 100 recipes and chose the best. My tasters included friends, neighbours and all members of my family who were very frank in their assessments and offered helpful suggestions about improving flavour. If flavour or texture didn't measure up to expectations, those recipes were discarded. The highlight for me on many occasions was when they said, "This isn't one of the low-salt dishes, is it?"

Most of these recipes are for main courses to add to the choices in *Delicious DASH Flavours*. They are grouped in seven categories to meet your mood and inclination:

Quick & easy skillet dishes
Main course salads
BBQ or broil
Slow & savoury entrées
Brunch or informal dinners
Simply elegant dinners
Pasta

To round out the dinner menu, there are side dishes of vegetables, grains and soups as well as desserts. Vegetarian dishes are included as well as ethnic food. So in addition to good down-home Canadian fare, you can choose from Chinese, Japanese, Malaysian, Thai, Indian and French. Ingredients for all these dishes are readily available in grocery stores.

Food author Michael Pollan advocates getting back to simpler whole foods with his mantra "Eat food. Not too much. Mostly plants." His philosophy of eating healthy, unprocessed food meshes well with the DASH eating plan.

DASH came out of a clinical study that tested the effects of nutrients in food on high blood pressure (hypertension). The study, an initiative of the US National Institutes of Health (NIH), showed that elevated blood pressure was reduced by eating a healthy diet emphasizing whole grains, fruits, vegetables and low-fat dairy foods while reducing the amount of meat, fat, cholesterol and sugar.

A second clinical study, DASH-Sodium, tested the theory that the DASH diet would work even better if it were low in salt. Salt contains sodium which influences the amount of fluid retained in our bodies, thus affecting blood pressure. Results showed that reducing dietary sodium lowered blood pressure, with the greatest benefit for those on the DASH eating plan with a sodium intake of 1,500 milligrams a day (equivalent to ⅔ tsp (3 mL) of table salt).

Most North American diets contain two to three times that amount of sodium and far more than the human body requires. The Canadian Heart and Stroke Foundation has reported that reducing salt would eliminate hypertension in one million Canadians. Hypertension is defined as a blood pressure reading of 140/90 or higher; prehypertension is 120/80 to 139/89.

Normal blood pressure is less than 120/80. Hypertension is a known risk factor for cardiovascular disease and heart attack. Studies have also found a link between high sodium levels and osteoporosis, diabetes and cancer.

Most of the salt in North American diets comes from processed food and restaurant meals with only 20% added during cooking or at the table. The *Wall Street Journal* reports that average sodium intake has increased about 50% since the 1970s because we are eating more convenience foods. As food processors have reduced fat and sugar in their products, they have often added more salt to restore flavour. Even fresh pork and chicken in the grocery store are sometimes "seasoned" by soaking in brine to make them more tender. In addition to increasing the sodium content, it also makes the meat heavier and adds to the price. If you feel bloated the day after eating out or notice that your rings are snugger than usual, it is likely a result of a high sodium meal and it will take a few days for your body to get rid of the "sodium load."

A 2009 article in the *Canadian Medical Association Journal* urges the Canadian government to increase its efforts in educating the public about the dangers of consuming too much salt. In 2007 Health Canada formed the Sodium Working Group including representatives from food manufacturing and food service industry groups, health-focused non-governmental organizations, the scientific community, consumer advocacy groups, health professional organizations and government. Their mandate is to develop and oversee the implementation of a strategy for reducing dietary sodium intake among Canadians. Doctors are concerned that government is not acting quickly enough.

The DASH eating plan is simple. In fact, it is nearly identical to Canada's Food Guide in the categories of food and number of servings. It differs mainly in requiring specific nutrients to help lower blood pressure naturally. Each day it recommends:

- 4700 mg of potassium, which can be found in vegetables (especially potatoes), fruit (bananas and apricots), grains, skim milk and meat.
- 1250 mg of calcium from skim milk, low-fat cheese and yogurt and leafy greens.
- 30 grams of fibre from grains, vegetables and fruits.
- no more than 1500 mg of sodium.

The success of DASH in reducing hypertension is attributed in part to these nutrients in natural foods such as grains, fruits, vegetables, low-fat dairy and modest amounts of meat that are naturally low in sodium and high in potassium. Potassium helps lower blood pressure by relaxing muscle cells in blood vessel walls, allowing blood vessels to expand. Blood pressure medications work in similar way. Potassium helps the body rid itself of sodium as well.

Researchers believe that naturally occurring phyto-nutrients in food also play important roles in regulating blood pressure. Phytonutrients, sometimes known as phytochemicals, are compounds found in fruits and vegetables that have benefits through their antioxidant and anti-inflammatory properties. They are also believed to protect against cancer and heart disease. Many of the bright colours and flavours in produce come from phytonutrients, such as anthocyanins in blueberries and beta carotene in carrots. Choose intensely coloured fruits and vegetables for greatest benefit.

MAKING THE TRANSITION TO DASH

The National Institutes of Health recommend that you make the change to the DASH eating plan gradually and begin by choosing foods low in sodium, low in saturated fat and low in calories. The tasty recipes in this book have been created to help you make an easy transition.

These are some strategies for making healthier dishes.

Treat meat as part of the meal, not the focus.
Combine smaller portions of meat with whole grain rice, pasta, barley or couscous.
Use fresh or frozen vegetables instead of canned ones, which contain salt.
Choose fresh meat and fish instead of the processed kind.
Cook whole-grain rice and pasta without salt.
Make soups and stocks from scratch as most commercial ones are high in salt.
Make your own seasoning mix: combine garlic powder, onion powder, black pepper, oregano and basil.
Avoid or reduce consumption of monosodium glutamate, sodium citrate, baking soda, baking powder and sodium bicarbonate.
Use low-fat cheeses or small amounts of aged cheeses for flavour.
Use small amounts of fat in cooking.
Eat fresh fruit for dessert or snacks.
Serve vegetables with chopped fresh herbs instead of butter.
Eat vegetarian dishes for a few meals each week.

In adapting recipes to DASH, I have made these substitutions:

Two egg whites for 1 whole egg
Sodium-free lemon pepper instead of salt
Fat-free or 1% yogurt instead of sour cream

In adapting recipes to the DASH eating plan, I added a variety of flavouring ingredients to tempt the palate. Herbs, spices and citrus impart more interesting flavours than salt does anyway.

Herbs spark up any dish and offer a great variety of flavours. Grow your own in your backyard or a pot on the window sill. They thrive even in poor soil and need a moderate amount of light. Perennials such as sage, oregano, chives, mint and French tarragon will come up year after year and require no care. Annuals such as basil, dill, thyme, summer savory and rosemary will grow until heavy frost hits them. If you can't grow your own, just pick up a bunch at the grocery store. Use what you need right away and preserve the rest by freezing or drying. I freeze basil, dill, tarragon, rosemary and chopped parsley in small plastic bags. Drying at room temperature works well for thyme, savory, sage and mint. You can't beat the flavour of stuffing made with fresh or freshly dried sage and savory.

Spices, whether whole or ground, will complement vegetable and meat dishes. Bay leaves are a must for soups and stock. Ground coriander, cumin, curry powder, turmeric and ginger add pungency. Don't forget freshly ground black pepper or green and pink peppercorns for variety. Fresh ginger root is a must in my kitchen. I peel a piece about 4 in (10 cm) long, cut it in several chunks and cover it with sherry in a covered glass jar. It will keep for months refrigerated. Fresh ginger, chili powder and cayenne pepper add heat to a dish. Cinnamon, cloves and allspice add a touch of sweetness, as does nutmeg. For best flavour, buy whole nutmeg and grate on a little grater whenever you need some.

Citrus can provide a burst of flavour in many dishes. The juice or grated zest of lemon, lime, orange or grapefruit will stimulate your taste buds.

Vinegar has a similar effect to citrus juice in lifting the flavour of food. There are so many varieties with different characteristics that I like to keep seven kinds on hand, ranging from mild to strong: rice vinegar, tarragon white wine vinegar, raspberry vinegar, cider vinegar, red wine vinegar, balsamic vinegar and white vinegar.

Vegetables that are aromatic add flavour and aroma, stimulating the senses. Garlic whether raw, sautéed or roasted is a wonderful flavour enhancer as are members of the onion family. Consider chives and green onions (chopped as an ingredient or used as a garnish), sweet Vidalia onions, red onions or leeks for salads, soups and stews. Onions can provide deep, rich flavours if they are caramelized (cooked slowly until browned). Celery adds both flavour and crunch.

Nuts and seeds are limited in DASH but in small amounts they add interest and texture as an ingredient or garnish. Flavour is enhanced by toasting them in the oven for a few minutes. Sesame seeds, poppy seeds and black onion seeds add to a dish when sprinkled on top. Mustard seeds, sautéed in a little oil until they pop, add flavour to curries.

The Heart and Stroke Foundation of Canada is a strong promoter of healthy eating and recommends DASH to reduce hypertension and strokes. They report that the Canadian Council of Food and Nutrition's survey on eating habits shows that the most significant change Canadians are making is to eat more servings of fruits and vegetables. Following even one part of the DASH diet such as eating more potassium-rich foods will help lower blood pressure. The more components of DASH that you follow, the more beneficial will be the effects on your health.

The easiest way to get started on the healthy DASH eating plan is to use the scrumptious recipes in this book as well as those in *Delicious DASH Flavours. Low-salt DASH Dinners* provides the following features:

Tasty recipes low in sodium, fat and cholesterol
Tested recipes that are easy to follow
Colourful photos of the dishes
Nutritional analyses for each recipe showing calories, fat, saturated fat, cholesterol, sodium, potassium, carbohydrates, sugar, fibre and protein
Comparison of DASH and Canada's Food Guide
Suggestions for making the transition to DASH
Summary of DASH Daily Nutritional Goals
Information about portion size
A sample menu for integrating DASH dinner recipes into the DASH eating plan
Tips for reducing salt and increasing potassium in your diet

Food author Michael Pollan claims that people are focused too much on the chemical makeup (nutrition) of food and not enough on the enjoyment of fresh, wholesome food. The philosophy of "good eating" involves an educational process. Once you understand the health benefits of natural, unrefined foods, you can enjoy them in your diet. The recipes in both of my DASH cookbooks have been thoughtfully created to be healthy, but enjoyment of the flavours, textures and presentation of the dishes is my top priority. You can indulge yourself using these recipes while knowing that you are doing your body a favour. Enjoy!

ACKNOWLEDGEMENTS

I want to thank the authors from whose books I selected recipes: Elaine Elliot and Virginia Lee, Brenda Matthews and Elizabeth Feltham. My appreciation also goes to friends who shared their special recipes: Carolyn Chipman, Mary Jane Covert, Richard Gonzalez, Dan Hatfield, Jessie Macdonald, Linda Macintosh, Helen Smith and Joy Tanton.

All recipes have been modified to meet the requirements of DASH and tested to ensure excellent flavour.

Thanks to Chef Michael Howell for his imaginative food styling, to photographer Jen Partridge and to Meghan Collins for art direction and props.

I am indebted to family and friends who tasted the prepared dishes and provided helpful feedback.

Claire Nowlan, M.D. provided helpful information on DASH.

QUICK & EASY
SKILLET DISHES

FIVE-SPICE CHICKEN AND BROCCOLI

Fresh ginger and garlic combine with Chinese five-spice powder to create an exotically flavoured dish.

Five-spice powder, available in Asian stores, is a combination of Chinese cinnamon (cassia), cloves, fennel seeds, Szechwan pepper or ginger, and star anise. Serve with Steamed White or Brown Rice (p. 143) or fine noodles.

1 lb (500 g) boneless, skinless chicken breasts cut into ¾-in (2-cm) cubes
1 tbsp (15 mL) oil
1 ½ tsp (7 mL) five-spice powder
¼ tsp (1 mL) cayenne pepper
1 slice ginger root about the size of a quarter, finely minced
2 tbsp (30 mL) low-sodium soy sauce
2 large stalks of broccoli
3 green onions, coarsely chopped
4 large mushrooms, sliced
2 cloves garlic, minced
1 cup (250 mL) water
1 tbsp (15 mL) cornstarch
2 tbsp (30 mL) water
1 tbsp (15 mL) sesame seeds

Sauté chicken cubes in ½ tbsp (7 mL) oil in a non-stick skillet over medium-high heat until lightly browned. Sprinkle with five-spice powder, cayenne, ginger and soy sauce and cook for a couple more minutes. Remove from pan.

Peel the tough outer skin from the broccoli and discard. Thinly slice stalks on the diagonal and separate the tops into florets.

Add remaining oil to the pan and stir-fry the broccoli, green onions, mushrooms and garlic over medium-high heat until tender crisp. Add 1 cup (250 mL) water and chicken. Bring to a boil, cover and simmer for 3 minutes. Mix cornstarch with 2 tbsp (30 mL) water. Add to pan and cook until thickened. Garnish with sesame seeds.

Serves 6.

Nutrient Analysis per serving:

Calories 149
Calories from Fat 38 (25%)
Total Fat 4g
Saturated Fat 1g
Cholesterol 44mg
Sodium 121mg
Potassium 526mg
Carbohydrates 8g
Fibre 1g
Sugar 1g
Protein 21g

NASI GORENG (MALAYSIAN FRIED RICE)

We were introduced to this dish in Malaysia where it is eaten any time of day. It is an excellent way to use leftover rice. Spice it up with sambal oelek, Asian hot pepper sauce, which is available at most supermarkets. I have tried different brands of brown basmati rice and find that Bulk Barn has the best — light and chewy, not gummy. Serve Nasi Goreng with small bowls of sambals such as roasted peanuts, cucumbers and chutney.

vegetable oil spray

2 egg whites, lightly beaten

½ tbsp (7 mL) olive oil

1 ¼ cups (310 mL) chopped onion

1 medium carrot cut in ¼-in (6-mm) dice

1 tsp (5 mL) ground cumin

½ tsp (2 mL) ground coriander

8 oz (250 g) chicken breast cut in ½-in (1.2-cm) dice

2 large cloves garlic, finely minced

½ cup (125 mL) chopped red pepper

1 tsp (5 mL) sambal oelek

3 cups (750 mL) cooked brown basmati rice, chilled

1 cup (250 mL) frozen peas

1 tbsp (15 mL) low-sodium soy sauce

1 cup (250 mL) cooked shrimp

¼ cup (60 mL) coarsely chopped cilantro

¼ cup (60 mL) roasted Spanish peanuts

1 cup (250 mL) English cucumber, seeded and cut into ¼-in (6-mm) dice

Heat a large non-stick skillet and spray lightly with vegetable oil. Pour in beaten egg whites and swirl to cover the bottom. Cook until firm, about a minute. Carefully flip egg and cook a few more seconds. Set aside on a plate to cool. When cool, roll up and cut into ⅛-in (3-mm) shreds. Set aside.

Return skillet to heat and add oil, onion and carrot. Stir-fry for about 4 minutes over medium-high heat. Stir in cumin, coriander, chicken, garlic and red pepper. Continue cooking for 4 minutes longer. Stir in sambal oelek, rice, peas and soy sauce and cook until hot.

Serve from skillet or transfer to a platter. Arrange shrimp on top of the rice. Garnish with shredded egg and cilantro. Serve with small bowls of peanuts and cucumber.

Serves 6, 1 cup (250 mL) each.

Nutrient Analysis per serving:	
Calories 280	Potassium 458mg
Calories from Fat 57 (20%)	Carbohydrates 36g
Total Fat 7g	Fibre 5g
Saturated Fat 1g	Sugar 3g
Cholesterol 43mg	Protein 20g
Sodium 189mg	

CHICKEN AND VEGGIE STIR-FRY WITH ALMONDS

Marinated chicken combined with colourful crisp vegetables and toasted almonds can be served over Steamed Brown Rice (p. 143). This dish uses low-sodium soy sauce, hoisin sauce and rice vinegar, a mild vinegar available at most grocery stores in the Asian foods section.

1 lb (500 g) boneless chicken breasts cut in 1-in (2.5-cm) cubes
1 tsp (5 mL) sherry
1 tsp (5 mL) low-sodium soy sauce
2 tsp (10 mL) cornstarch
6 dried shitake mushrooms
2 stalks celery
1 medium carrot, peeled
1 cup (250 mL) red and/or green peppers, cut into 1-in (2.5-cm) cubes
6 fresh mushrooms, sliced
2 cloves garlic, minced
1 or 2 tbsp (15 or 30 mL) fresh ginger cut into very fine julienne
1 tbsp (15 mL) olive oil, divided
2 tsp (10 mL) cornstarch
¾ cup (175 mL) water
1 tbsp (15 mL) rice vinegar
1 tbsp (15 mL) low-sodium soy sauce
1 tbsp (15 mL) hoisin sauce
¼ cup (60 mL) whole toasted almonds

Combine chicken, sherry, soy sauce and 2 tsp (10 mL) cornstarch in a small bowl and marinate for 5 minutes.

Immerse dried shitake mushrooms in hot water for 5 minutes or until softened. Drain well. Remove and discard tough stems. Cut mushrooms into thin slices.

Cut celery and carrot into sticks 2 in (5 cm) long and ¼ in (6 mm) wide. Combine with shitake mushrooms, peppers, fresh mushrooms, garlic and ginger and set aside.

Place a large skillet or wok over high heat. Add ½ tbsp (7mL) oil and the chicken and stir-fry until the chicken is browned on all sides. Remove from the pan to a bowl.

Add remaining ½ tbsp (7 mL) oil to the pan and place over medium-high heat. Add all the vegetables and stir-fry for 3 minutes. Cover and continue cooking 2 minutes or until tender crisp.

Mix cornstarch with about 2 tbsp (30 mL) of the water. Whisk in remaining water, vinegar, soy sauce and hoisin sauce and add to vegetables. Cook and stir until thickened. Stir in chicken and cook until heated through. Sprinkle toasted almonds on top and serve at once over steamed brown basmati rice.

Serves 6, 1 cup (250 mL) each.

Nutrient Analysis per serving:	
Calories 116	Potassium 409mg
Calories from Fat 48 (42%)	Carbohydrates 13g
Total Fat 6g	Fibre 3g
Saturated Fat 1g	Sugar 4g
Cholesterol 7mg	Protein 6g
Sodium 121mg	

CHICKEN CURRY WITH APRICOTS AND ALMONDS

The secret to the rich flavour of this delectable golden curry is the addition of ground almonds to the sauce. Give it an extra bite with a sprinkle of cayenne pepper. Serve over Steamed Brown Rice (p. 143) with extra yogurt on the side.

½ cup (125 mL) dried apricots
1 tbsp (15 mL) olive oil, divided
1 ½ lb (750 g) boneless, skinless chicken breasts cut into several pieces
freshly ground pepper
2 tbsp (30 mL) fresh ginger, finely minced
2 large garlic cloves, finely minced
1 large onion, finely chopped
1 ½ tbsp (22 mL) curry powder
½ cup (125 mL) ground almonds
2 cups (500 mL) water
1 tsp (5 mL) Worcestershire sauce
3 tbsp (45 mL) fat-free yogurt
2 green onions, thinly sliced

Soak apricots in boiling water in a small bowl until softened, about 15 minutes: drain.

Heat half the olive oil in a large non-stick skillet and sauté chicken breasts over medium-high heat until lightly browned on each side. Season with pepper and transfer to a plate.

Add remaining olive oil to the pan along with ginger, garlic and onion and cook over medium-low heat for 8 minutes. Add curry powder and continue cooking for a few more minutes, stirring to be sure curry doesn't scorch.

Add ground almonds, water and Worcestershire sauce and bring to a boil, stirring to scrape brown bits from the bottom of the pan. Reduce heat to simmer and add chicken breasts and apricots. Cover and simmer for about 10 minutes.

Transfer chicken to a serving platter and keep warm. Boil sauce until thickened, about 6 minutes. Stir in yogurt and pour sauce over chicken. Scatter green onions over top and serve at once.

Serves 6.

Nutrient Analysis per serving:	
Calories 169	Potassium 435mg
Calories from Fat 77 (46%)	Carbohydrates 16g
Total Fat 9g	Fibre 2g
Saturated Fat 1g	Sugar 2g
Cholesterol 11mg	Protein 8g
Sodium 35mg	

HALIBUT WITH MUSHROOMS, TOMATOES AND ARTICHOKES

The Compass Rose Inn, Lunenburg, NS

Halibut is a delicious fish of the North Atlantic with firm white flesh and mild flavour. The addition of mushrooms, fresh tomatoes and artichokes adds extra flair. The original recipe was made with demi-glace brown sauce, but it has been omitted as it is too high in sodium for the DASH diet.

4 tsp (20 mL) olive oil
4 halibut steaks or fillets, each 5 oz (140 g)
2 cups (500 mL) sliced mushrooms
1 or 2 cloves garlic, minced
4 canned artichoke hearts, quartered
2 cups (500 mL) peeled and diced tomatoes
½ cup (125 mL) parsley, chopped
juice of a lemon
freshly ground pepper

Heat 2 tsp (10 mL) of the olive oil in a skillet, and sauté halibut until just cooked, approximately 7 to 10 minutes depending upon thickness of fish. Fish is cooked when it flakes easily and is opaque.

Sauté mushrooms, garlic and artichokes in remaining oil in another skillet. Add tomatoes and parsley to the skillet and simmer for about 5 minutes. Squeeze lemon juice over halibut and season with pepper. To serve, arrange halibut on plates and top with mushroom sauce.

Serves 4.

Nutrient Analysis per serving:

Calories 234	Sodium 110mg
Calories from Fat 72 (31%)	Potassium 1092mg
Total Fat 8g	Carbohydrates 8g
Saturated Fat 1g	Fibre 3g
Cholesterol 45mg	Protein 32g

CHINESE BEEF AND TOMATO WITH PEPPERS AND ONIONS

This colourful, classic Cantonese dish, while simple to make, is packed with flavour from pepper, onion and fresh tomatoes seasoned with ginger and garlic. Serve with Steamed White Rice (p. 143).

8 oz (250 g) sirloin or other tender steak
1 tsp (5 mL) cornstarch
1 tsp (5 mL) low-sodium soy sauce
½ tsp (2 mL) honey
2 tsp (10 mL) sherry
4 tsp (20 mL) oil
slice of fresh ginger, size of a quarter, peeled and minced
1 green pepper, cut in 1-in (2.5-cm) pieces
2 onions, cut lengthwise into thin wedges
2 cloves garlic, minced
6 oz (170 mL) Golden Vegetable Broth (p.155) or water
2 tsp (10 mL) cornstarch
2 tsp (10 mL) cold water
1 tbsp (15 mL) low-sodium soy sauce
3 large or 4 medium tomatoes, each cut into 8 wedges
1 tbsp (15 mL) sesame seeds

Slice steak into thin strips and mix with 1 tsp (5 mL) each cornstarch, soy sauce plus honey and sherry.

Heat large skillet or wok until very hot. Add half the oil, marinated steak strips and minced ginger. Stir-fry until browned and remove to a bowl.

Reheat pan and add remaining oil along with green pepper, onions and garlic. Stir-fry for 3 minutes. Add broth and bring to a boil. Cover and simmer for 2 minutes.

Meanwhile combine cornstarch, water and soy sauce. Add cooked beef and cornstarch mixture to vegetables, cooking and stirring until sauce is thick and clear. Stir in tomato wedges. Serve with fluffy steamed white rice, garnished with sesame seeds.

Serves 6.

Nutrient Analysis per serving:	
Calories 142	Potassium 465mg
Calories from Fat 55 (39%)	Carbohydrates 12g
Total Fat 6g	Fibre 2g
Saturated Fat 1g	Sugar 6g
Cholesterol 16mg	Protein 10g
Sodium 61mg	

SICILIAN CHICKEN

Bluenose Lodge, Lunenburg, NS

Arab invaders brought the first citrus trees to Sicily in the ninth century and since that time orange groves have thrived all over the island, imparting the scent of orange blossoms. This elegant dish captures some of that essence as fresh oranges, sweet vermouth and a touch of oregano combine with juicy chicken breasts in a healthy, low-fat treat. Serve with Four-Grain Pilaf with Currents and Cranberries (p.142).

¼ cup (60 mL) whole-wheat flour
¼ tsp (1 mL) salt-free lemon pepper
1 tbsp (15 mL) fresh parsley, chopped
½ tsp (2 mL) paprika
¼ tsp (1 mL) dried oregano
4 boneless chicken breasts, 4 oz (125 g) each
1 tbsp (15 mL) olive oil
8 slices fresh orange
¾ cup (175 mL) fresh orange juice
¼ cup (60 mL) sweet vermouth

Make seasoned flour by combining flour, pepper, parsley, paprika and oregano. Dredge chicken breasts in the seasoned flour.

Heat oil in a skillet and add breasts, sautéing on both sides until golden and almost cooked. Cover each breast with 2 slices of orange and add orange juice. Cover and cook 3 minutes. Remove breasts from skillet and keep warm.

Boil juice in the skillet to reduce it to about ⅓ cup (75 mL). Add vermouth and reduce slightly. Serve chicken with cooked orange slices or with fresh ones, if you prefer, topped with the orange-vermouth sauce.

Serves 4.

Nutrient Analysis per serving:

Calories 272	Potassium 523mg
Calories from Fat 46 (17%)	Carbohydrates 19g
Total Fat 5g	Fibre 2g
Saturated Fat 1g	Sugar 8g
Cholesterol 66mg	Protein 28g
Sodium 84mg	

HADDOCK FILLETS WITH PEACH AND PEPPER SALSA

Bluenose Lodge, Lunenburg, NS

Grace Swan of the Bluenose Lodge uses colourful Peach and Pepper Salsa to turn a fish fillet into a gourmet feast. She coats the fillets with breadcrumbs and sautés them in butter. I changed the coating to whole-wheat flour and toasted coconut and sautéed them in extra virgin olive oil. To reduce cholesterol, use 2 egg whites instead of the whole egg. Serve this dish with Honeyed Carrots in Grand Marnier (p. 139), green beans and rice. Serve garnished with Peach & Pepper Salsa (p. 146).

1 ¼ lb (625 g) fillet of haddock (or white fish of choice)
1 egg, beaten
1 tsp (5 mL) low-sodium soy sauce
1 tbsp (15 mL) water
¼ cup (60 mL) whole-wheat flour
2 tbsp (30 mL) toasted coconut
freshly ground pepper, to taste
1 tbsp (15 mL) olive oil

Cut haddock into 4 serving pieces, being careful to remove any bones. Combine egg, soy sauce and water. Combine whole-wheat flour and coconut on a piece of waxed paper. Dip fish in egg mixture, coat with flour mixture and season with pepper.

Heat half the oil in a non-stick skillet and cook fillets until golden on one side. Add remaining oil and turn the fish, cooking until fish flakes and is opaque.

Serves 4.

Nutrient Analysis per serving:

Calories 123	Potassium 203mg
Calories from Fat 54 (44%)	Carbohydrates 6g
Total Fat 6g	Fibre 1g
Saturated Fat 2g	Sugar 0g
Cholesterol 47mg	Protein 11g
Sodium 53mg	

NORTH AFRICAN COUSCOUS PAELLA WITH SHRIMP AND CHICKEN

This is an adaptation of a dish in Moosewood Restaurant Cooks at Home *that can be prepared in 20 minutes. Use whole-wheat couscous for a nutty flavour and higher fibre than regular couscous. Serve garnished with lemon wedges or slices of Asian pear arranged to form a flower.*

½ tbsp (7 mL) olive oil
8 oz (250 g) chicken breast, cubed
½ cup (125 mL) chopped sweet red pepper
½ cup (125 mL) chopped green onions
2 cloves of garlic, minced
1 tsp (5 mL) ground coriander
½ tsp (2 mL) turmeric
½ tsp (2 mL) ground cumin
2 tsp (10 mL) Patak's mild curry paste
¼ tsp (1 mL) cayenne, optional
1 ¾ cups (425 mL) hot vegetable broth or water
1 tbsp (15 mL) lemon juice
1 cup (250 mL) fresh or frozen peas, thawed
¼ cup (60 mL) dry currants or golden raisins
1 cup (250 mL) whole-wheat couscous
freshly ground pepper
8 oz (250 mL) cooked shelled shrimp
¼ cup (60 mL) sliced almonds, toasted
½ cup (125 mL) chopped cilantro or parsley
lemon wedges or pear (optional for garnish)

Heat oil in a 2 quart (2 L) heavy saucepan. Add chicken cubes and sauté until golden. Stir in pepper, onions, garlic, coriander, turmeric, cumin, curry paste and cayenne; cook over medium heat for 4 minutes, stirring occasionally. Stir in broth and lemon juice and bring to a boil. Add peas and currants and cook for a minute. Mix in couscous; cover, remove from heat and let stand for 5 minutes.

Uncover pan and fluff with a fork, breaking up any lumps. Season with pepper and more lemon juice, if desired. Stir in shrimp or scatter them over top.

Serve on a platter, topped with toasted almonds and cilantro or parsley.

Serves 6, 1 ⅓ cup (325 mL) each.

Nutrient Analysis per serving:	
Calories 275	Potassium 396mg
Calories from Fat 59 (21%)	Carbohydrates 32g
Total Fat 7g	Fibre 6g
Saturated Fat 1g	Sugar 3g
Cholesterol 79mg	Protein 24g
Sodium 164mg	

CHICKEN KORMA

Chicken flavoured with the exotic spices of India and braised in yogurt makes a moist, tender and delectable dish. The flavour is even better the second day, so we always look forward to leftovers. A garnish of lemon wedges adds to the presentation. Serve over Steamed White Rice (p. 143).

1 ½ lb (750 g) boneless, skinless chicken breasts
3 onions
1 tbsp (15 mL) olive oil
½ jalapeño or chili pepper or ¼ tsp (1 mL) dried red pepper seeds
1 tbsp (15 mL) finely minced fresh ginger
1 tbsp (15 mL) ground cumin
1 tsp (5 mL) ground coriander
½ tsp (2 mL) ground turmeric
1 tbsp (15 mL) shredded coconut
2 cardamom pods, crushed or ¼ tsp (1 mL) ground cardamom
2 tbsp (30 mL) sultana raisins
1 tomato, finely diced
1 ¼ cups (310 mL) plain fat-free yogurt
fresh lemon juice to taste

Cut chicken breasts into 1-in (2.5-cm) dice. Thinly slice two of the onions and set the other aside for later.

Heat oil in a large heavy pan; add hot pepper and sliced onions. Sauté until they begin to brown.

Chop remaining onion and add it to the pan with ginger, cumin, coriander, turmeric and coconut. Sauté for a couple of minutes while stirring to allow the spices to cook. Add chicken, cardamom and sultanas and continue cooking for a few minutes.

Add tomato and half the yogurt; simmer uncovered until chicken is cooked. Stir in remaining yogurt and lemon juice; heat but do not boil.

Serves 6.

Nutrient Analysis per serving:

Calories 243	Potassium 614mg
Calories from Fat 56 (23%)	Carbohydrates 16g
Total Fat 6g	Fibre 2g
Saturated Fat 3g	Sugar 6g
Cholesterol 69mg	Protein 30g
Sodium 116mg	

MAIN COURSE
SALADS

WARM SCALLOP AND PORTABELLO MUSHROOM SALAD

The Schoolhouse Country Inn Restaurant, Belwood, ON

Chef Peter Egger has created this delicious and attractive warm salad that he recommends serving as a light summer lunch or dinner main course. Balsamic vinegar accentuates the sweetness of fresh scallops and I have added red pepper for a dash of colour. This recipe uses fresh ginger, which you can keep in your fridge for weeks by peeling it and immersing it in sherry in a small screw-cap jar.

1 ½ tbsp (22 mL) olive oil
4 large Portobello mushrooms, thinly sliced
½ sweet red pepper, cut into thin slivers
1 clove garlic, minced
1 tbsp (15 mL) minced fresh ginger root
1 shallot or 2 green onions, finely chopped
1 lb (500 g) fresh scallops
4 tbsp (60 mL) balsamic vinegar
6 cups (1.5 L) mixed salad greens
1 sprig fresh thyme
freshly ground pepper
4 tbsp (60 mL) chopped cilantro or parsley

Heat oil over medium-high heat in a skillet; sauté mushrooms, pepper, garlic, ginger and shallots until tender. Add scallops and balsamic vinegar; cook just until scallops are firm and opaque.

Arrange greens in the centre of 4 plates. Using a slotted spoon and reserving liquid in the skillet, transfer scallops and vegetables to top of greens.

Add thyme and pepper to liquid in skillet and bring to a boil to reduce slightly. Drizzle liquid over salad and sprinkle cilantro on top.

Serves 4.

Nutrient Analysis per serving:	
Calories 278	Potassium 1739mg
Calories from Fat 59 (21%)	Carbohydrates 32g
Total Fat 7g	Fibre 4g
Saturated Fat 1g	Sugar 4g
Cholesterol 34mg	Protein 24g
Sodium 213mg	

CAROLYN'S MEDITERRANEAN PASTA SALAD

There are many tasty recipes for pasta salad, but this one is tops with me. Carolyn Chipman combines multi-coloured rotini pasta with a variety of crisp vegetables and feta cheese to create a salad that is the star of the buffet table. It is perfect for large gatherings in the summer as it makes 16 servings.

12 oz (375 g) rainbow fusilli
3 tbsp (45 mL) extra virgin olive oil
3 tbsp (45 mL) fresh lemon juice
2 tbsp (30 mL) pasta cooking water
3 cloves garlic, chopped
1 tsp (5 mL) dried basil or 4 tbsp (60 mL) fresh basil
½ cup (125 mL) low-fat feta cheese, crumbled
2 tomatoes, diced
1 English cucumber, diced
8 radishes, thinly sliced
1 red or green pepper, chopped
4 green onions, chopped
1 cup (250 mL) chopped parsley
freshly ground pepper
dry crumbled oregano, optional
4 Greek Kalamata black olives, cut into slivers
1 large tomato cut into wedges for garnish

Cook fusilli according to package instructions. Drain, reserving some of the cooking water, and cool. Transfer pasta to a large bowl.

Prepare dressing in a blender by combining oil, lemon juice, cooking water, garlic and basil and blend until smooth. (I used fresh basil cut into very fine shreds and added to the dressing after it was blended.)

Add dressing to pasta and toss gently to mix. Add feta cheese and remaining vegetables except olives and fold into pasta. Adjust seasoning with pepper and oregano.

Transfer to serving bowl and garnish with olives and tomato wedges.

Serves 16.

Nutrient Analysis per serving:	
Calories 118	Potassium 173mg
Calories from Fat 29 (25%)	Carbohydrates 19g
Total Fat 3g	Fibre 1g
Saturated Fat 1g	Sugar 1g
Cholesterol <1mg	Protein 3g
Sodium 25mg	

GREEN SALAD OLE WITH CHILI-GLAZED SHRIMP

This fruit-studded salad, topped with Chili-Glazed Shrimp and feta cheese, makes a perfect luncheon dish. It can be prepared in a large bowl or as individual servings, which I prefer. You can replace the oranges and grapefruit with 2 peeled and diced mangoes or papaya for variety. Toast sesame seeds in a small skillet for a few minutes over medium heat until they start to colour.

Green Salad

¼ cup (60 mL) orange juice
1 tsp (5 mL) grated orange zest
1 tbsp (15 mL) cider or rice vinegar
1 tsp (5 mL) olive oil
1 tsp (5 mL) honey
⅛ tsp (½ mL) dried crushed red pepper flakes
8 cups (2 L) torn romaine or spinach leaves
2 grapefruit, peeled and cut into sections
2 oranges, peeled and cut into sections
1 small red pepper, seeded and cut into thin slivers
½ cup (125 mL) low-fat feta cheese, crumbled
1 tbsp (15 mL) toasted sesame seeds

Chili-Glazed Shrimp

8 oz (250 g) large raw shrimp
½ cup (125 mL) orange juice
3 or 4 cloves garlic, minced
1 tsp (5 mL) chili powder

For the salad:
Prepare dressing by whisking together orange juice and zest, vinegar, oil, honey and pepper flakes. Set aside.

Place romaine in serving dishes and arrange fruit and red pepper slivers to form a pinwheel pattern. Drizzle dressing over the salad. Top with glazed shrimp and feta cheese and sprinkle with sesame seeds

For the shrimp:
Peel and devein shrimp; set aside.

To make the glaze, combine orange juice, garlic and chili powder in a non-stick skillet and bring to a boil over high heat. Boil for a few minutes while stirring until mixture forms a thick glaze in the bottom of the pan. Reduce heat to medium and add shrimp, stirring to coat with the glaze. Cook for a few minutes until shrimp are done. Add a bit of water if glaze becomes too thick.

Serves 4.

Nutrient Analysis per serving:

Calories 231	Potassium 839mg
Calories from Fat 39 (17%)	Carbohydrates 36g
Total Fat 4g	Fibre 7g
Saturated Fat 1g	Sugar 22g
Cholesterol 87mg	Protein 16g
Sodium 118mg	

SPINACH SUNSHINE SALAD

Fern Resort, Orillia, ON

This healthy, low-sodium salad, filled with fruits and vegetables, makes a perfect summer lunch. Executive Chef Simon Le Henaff calls it a "sunshine" salad because of its delightful array of colourful fruit.

Spinach Sunshine Salad

2 10-oz (280-g) packages fresh spinach
2 cups (500 mL) sliced button mushrooms
2 kiwis, sliced
1 10-oz (280-g) can mandarin oranges, drained
½ cup (125 mL) sliced peaches
½ cup (125 mL) sliced mango
1 English cucumber, sliced
12 strawberries

Raspberry Vinaigrette

¼ cup (60 mL) raspberry vinegar
¼ cup (60 mL) apple juice or orange juice
1 tbsp (15 mL) honey
½ tsp (2 mL) grainy or old-fashioned Dijon mustard
¼ tsp (1 mL) freshly ground pepper
2 tbsp (30 mL) extra virgin olive oil
1 clove garlic, crushed, not chopped

For the salad:
Wash, dry and stem spinach; tear into bite-size pieces. Combine spinach, mushrooms, kiwis, mandarin oranges, peaches, mangoes and cucumber in a large bowl. Drizzle with raspberry vinaigrette; toss gently. Cover and refrigerate until chilled.

To serve, arrange salad attractively on 6 plates. Garnish each with 2 strawberries sliced and spread apart slightly to form fan.

For the vinaigrette:
Whisk the first 6 ingredients together: then add the crushed garlic. Let stand for a few minutes. Remove garlic before pouring the dressing over the salad.

Serves 6.

Nutrient Analysis per serving:

Calories 158	Potassium 984mg
Calories from Fat 47 (30%)	Carbohydrates 27g
Total Fat 5g	Fibre 5g
Saturated Fat 1g	Sugar 17g
Cholesterol 0mg	Protein 5g
Sodium 87mg	

JOY'S SPINACH AND RICE SALAD

Joy Tanton brought this divine salad to a potluck lunch to mark the closing of our Ladies' Fitness Class and it was an immediate hit. It is colourful with interesting textures, and is a meal in itself. I make it with brown basmati rice and wild rice for a nutty flavour. (To cook rice, rinse and drain ½ cup (125 mL) brown rice and ¼ cup (60 mL) wild rice; bring to a boil with 2 cups (500 mL) water and simmer covered for about 40 to 45 minutes. Cool rice before using.) Joy sometimes replaces the red pepper with shredded carrots.

Spinach and Rice Salad
2 cups (500 mL) cooked rice
2 cups (500 mL) fresh bean sprouts
3 stalks celery, finely chopped
6 cups (1.5 L) baby spinach, chopped
⅓ cup (75 mL) golden raisins
1 cup (250 mL) sliced white mushrooms
1 small red pepper, finely sliced
½ cup (125 mL) or more chopped parsley
½ cup (125 mL) chopped green onions

Dressing
3 tbsp (45 mL) low-sodium soy sauce
2 or 3 cloves garlic, minced
2 ½ tbsp (37 mL) olive oil
1 tbsp (15 mL) water
1 tbsp (15 mL) sesame oil
freshly ground pepper to taste
½ cup (125 mL) sliced almonds, toasted

For the salad:
Combine rice, sprouts, celery, spinach, raisins, mushrooms, pepper, parsley and onions in a salad bowl.

For the dressing:
Prepare dressing by shaking together in a jar the soy sauce, garlic, olive oil, water, sesame oil and ground pepper.

Toss salad with dressing just before serving and sprinkle almonds over top.

Serves 8.

Nutrient Analysis per serving:	
Calories 191	Potassium 431mg
Calories from Fat 87 (46%)	Carbohydrates 23g
Total Fat 10g	Fibre 4g
Saturated Fat 1g	Sugar 7g
Cholesterol 0mg	Protein 5g
Sodium 99mg	

JAPANESE STYLE SALMON AND EDAMAME SALAD

This delicious, healthy salad made from salmon and edamame is an excellent source of omega-3 and protein. Edamame are bright green soybeans available frozen in their pods. Just thaw and shell them for this salad. We were seved a bowl of fresh edamame as an appetizer in Japan. Wasabi is a very hot Japanese horseradish sold in tubes for convenience.

8 oz (250 g) poached salmon*
2 stalks celery, finely diced
1 cup (250 mL) shelled edamame
2 green onions, thinly sliced
4 tbsp (60 mL) low-fat mayonnaise
4 tbsp (60 mL) fat-free yogurt
2 tsp (10 mL) fresh lemon juice
1 tsp (5 mL) wasabi
freshly ground black pepper
4 cups (1 L) mixed greens
1 ½ tbsp (22 mL) fine julienned fresh ginger or pink sushi ginger
1 tbsp (15 mL) toasted sesame seeds

* To poach salmon, put it in a pan and cover with water. Add a bay leaf and squeeze of lemon. Bring to a boil and simmer for 5 to 10 minutes until cooked. Remove salmon from water and cool to room temperature

Flake salmon and combine with celery, edamame and green onions in a bowl. To make the dressing, whisk together mayonnaise, yogurt, lemon juice and wasabi in a small bowl. Fold into salmon mixture and season with pepper.

Arrange greens on 4 plates and mound salmon mixture on top. Garnish with ginger and sesame seeds.

Serves 4.

Nutrient Analysis per serving:	
Calories 265	Potassium 712mg
Calories from Fat 144 (54%)	Carbohydrates 11g
Total Fat 17g	Fibre 5g
Saturated Fat 3g	Sugar 2g
Cholesterol 39mg	Protein 21g
Sodium 208mg	

LENTIL, WILD RICE AND ORZO SALAD

This recipe, adapted from Canadian Living 20th Anniversary Cookbook, *is wonderful with barbecued meat and fish or on a buffet table. The wild rice, lentils, currants and almonds give it an interesting texture and the combination of spices evokes a Moroccan theme. Orzo is pasta shaped like rice. Wild rice has a longer cooking time than lentils, so it is cooked first and then lentils are cooked in the same water. This dish is ideal for entertaining a crowd as it serves 12 and you can make it ahead of time. Serve it warm or at room temperature. Add chopped green onion or parsley for variety.*

Salad
⅔ cup (150 mL) wild rice
1 cup (250 mL) green or brown lentils
⅔ cup (150 mL) orzo pasta
½ cup (125 mL) currants
⅓ cup (75 mL) chopped dates
¼ cup (60 mL) red onion, finely chopped
½ cup (125 mL) celery, finely chopped
⅓ cup (75 mL) slivered almonds, toasted

Dressing
¼ cup (60 mL) tarragon white wine vinegar
1 clove garlic, minced
1 tsp (5 mL) ground cumin
1 tsp (5 mL) Dijon mustard
1 tsp (5 mL) low-sodium soy sauce
1 tsp (5 mL) balsamic vinegar
½ tsp (2 mL) each honey, ground coriander
¼ tsp (1 mL) freshly ground black pepper
½ tsp (2 mL) each turmeric, paprika, nutmeg, ground cardamom
pinch of cinnamon, cloves, cayenne
2 tbsp (30 mL) olive oil

For the salad:
Cook wild rice in 8 cups (2 L boiling water in a large covered pot until tender, about 40 to 45 minutes. Drain rice and add to a large bowl, reserving the water to cook lentils.

Return cooking liquid to the pot and add washed and drained lentils. Bring to a boil and simmer for about 15 minutes or until tender. Don't overcook or they will be mushy. Drain lentils and add to rice.

Cook orzo according to package instructions. Drain well and add to large bowl with currants, dates, onion and celery.

Pour dressing over rice mixture and toss gently. Let salad cool to room temperature. Sprinkle with almonds and serve. Salad can be refrigerated for up to 2 days.

For the dressing:
Whisk all ingredients together to blend.

Serves 12, ⅔ cup (150 mL) each.

Nutrient Analysis per serving:

Calories 201	Potassium 344mg
Calories from Fat 41 (21%)	Carbohydrates 33g
Total Fat 5g	Fibre 7g
Saturated Fat 1g	Sugar 9g
Cholesterol 0mg	Protein 8g
Sodium 28mg	

BBQ OR
BROIL

BARBECUED BEEF SIRLOIN AND BLACK BEAN BURGERS

This burger has a great beefy flavour and the nutrition content is boosted with the addition of black beans and brown rice. You can alter seasonings to suit your taste. Instead of cumin and coriander, try 1 tsp (5 mL) each oregano and basil or fresh savory and sage. For a French twist, add ¼ cup (60 mL) dry red wine and 2 tbsp (30 mL) each of fresh thyme and minced shallots. Serve prepared mustard with horseradish as a tangy condiment for extra bite. Choose whole-wheat or whole-grain burger buns and be sure to check sodium content as many breads contain a liberal dose of salt.

1 cup (250 mL) cooked black beans
1 lb (500 g) lean ground beef sirloin
½ cup (125 mL) cooked and cooled brown rice
1 ½ tsp (7 mL) ground cumin
1 ½ tsp (7 mL) ground coriander
1 tsp (5 mL) chili powder
freshly ground pepper
garlic powder
6 whole-wheat burger buns
1 ripe avocado, peeled, seeded and sliced
6 slices sweet onion
6 slices tomato
6 lettuce leaves

In a large bowl, mash black beans slightly and combine with ground beef, brown rice, cumin, coriander and chili powder. Mix well and form into 6 patties using wet hands. Sprinkle generously with pepper and garlic powder. Cook on a heated barbecue or in a large skillet over medium-high heat until browned and done in the centre.

Serve on warmed buns topped with avocado, onion, tomato slices and lettuce leaves.

Serves 6.

Nutrient Analysis per serving:

Calories 335	Potassium 1094mg
Calories from Fat 102 (30%)	Carbohydrates 36g
Total Fat 11g	Fibre 8g
Saturated Fat 2g	Sugar 6g
Cholesterol 33mg	Protein 24g
Sodium 206mg	

BEEF TENDERLOIN WITH STILTON AND MIXED GREENS

Pickerel Lake Lodge, Burk's Falls, ON

Executive Chef Augustyn Merkies created this attractive dish that is perfect for easy summer entertaining. Beef steaks are marinated for several hours or overnight to add depth and subtlety to the flavour as well as to tenderize them. To reduce fat, I changed Chef Merkies's recipe by replacing olive oil with red wine. Instead of Stilton cheese, I used award-winning artisanal Dragon's Breath surface-ripened blue cheese from That Dutchman's Farm in Nova Scotia.

Marinade
½ cup (125 mL) wine
1 tbsp (15 mL) olive oil
1 tbsp (15 mL) low-sodium soy sauce
2 tsp (10 mL) dry mustard
2 tsp (10 mL) paprika
1 ½ tsp (7 mL) dried rosemary or thyme
1 ½ tsp (7 mL) dried basil
2 tsp (10 mL) finely minced fresh garlic
1 tsp (5 mL) onion powder
1 tsp (5 mL) black pepper
½ tsp (2 mL) white pepper

Meat and vegetables
6 beef tenderloin steaks, each 4 oz (125 g)
6 Portobello mushrooms, stems removed
2 sweet red peppers, each cut into 12 strips
6 cups (1.5 L) mixed greens or mesclun mix
3 tbsp (45 mL) Stilton or Dragon's Breath cheese

Combine marinade ingredients in a glass dish large enough to hold meat and vegetables. Add steaks to the marinade, turning to coat well. Add mushrooms and peppers and brush with marinade. Cover and refrigerate for several hours or overnight.

Transfer steaks to greased grill over high heat; cook to desired doneness. Remove from grill; let stand for 5 minutes before slicing across the grain ¼ in (6 mm) thick. Grill mushrooms and red pepper strips until tender and grill marks appear. Slice mushrooms ¼ in (6 mm) thick.

Arrange mixed greens in centre of 6 plates. Arrange grilled vegetables attractively over greens and top with steak slices. Crumble cheese over top.

Serves 6.

Nutrient Analysis per serving:

Calories 288	Potassium 1417mg
Calories from Fat 105 (36%)	Carbohydrates 14g
Total Fat 11g	Fibre 5g
Saturated Fat 4g	Sugar 5g
Cholesterol 79mg	Protein 31g
Sodium 155mg	

GRILLED STRIPLOIN WITH BUTTERNUT SQUASH, CUMIN AND LIME CONDIMENT

Keltic Lodge, Ingonish Beach, NS

Executive Chef Dale Nichols has created a tangy squash condiment to serve with steak. He also recommends serving it with halibut and salmon.

Condiment
4 tsp (20 mL) canola oil, portioned
1 cup (250 mL) diced red onion
¾ lb (375 g) butternut squash (or squash of choice),
   peeled and finely diced
½ tbsp (7 mL) minced garlic
1 tbsp (15 mL) ground cumin
¼ cup (60 mL) water
2 tbsp (30 mL) molasses
2 tbsp (30 mL) fresh orange juice
2 tbsp (30 mL) red wine vinegar
1 lime, cut in half
½ cup (125 mL) roughly chopped parsley or cilantro

Steaks
6 strip loin steaks 1 in (2.5 cm) thick, each 5 oz (140 g)
2 tbsp (30 mL) mixed peppercorns, crushed
vegetable oil spray

For the condiment:
Heat 2 tsp (10 mL) oil in a large saucepan over medium heat; add onion and sauté, stirring occasionally, until translucent, about 6 minutes. Remove onion from pan and reserve.

Return saucepan to heat; add remaining oil and heat until hot but not smoking. Add squash and sauté, stirring occasionally, until browned, about 5 minutes. Add reserved onion to pan along with garlic and cumin. Sauté, stirring frequently, for 1 minute.

Add water, molasses, orange juice and vinegar; bring to a simmer. Cook partially covered. Stir occasionally, until squash is tender but not overcooked, about 10 minutes. Remove squash from heat; squeeze lime juice on mixture, sprinkle with parsley, and stir to combine. Cover and keep warm while preparing the steaks.

For the steaks:
Heat a grill or barbecue. Season steaks with a generous coating of crushed peppercorns and spray with vegetable oil. Cook steaks on a hot barbecue or grill, turning once during the cooking — about 5 minutes for rare, 8 minutes for medium, and 12 minutes for well-done.

To serve, arrange steaks on warmed plates, top with a large spoonful of squash condiment.

Serves 6.

Nutrient Analysis per serving:	
Calories 281	Potassium 893mg
Calories from Fat 83 (29%)	Carbohydrates 18g
Total Fat 9g	Fibre 3g
Saturated Fat 3g	Sugar 6g
Cholesterol 75mg	Protein 34g
Sodium 92mg	

HERB-BAKED SALMON

Elaine Elliot and Virginia Lee

The key to this fragrant baked salmon is the mixture of fresh herbs: parsley, thyme, tarragon and rosemary. It is a wonderful way to prepare a whole salmon for a group. It can be barbecued as well as baked.

3 lb (1.5 kg) salmon, preferably deboned
4 tbsp (60 mL) fresh lemon juice
vegetable oil spray
¼ tsp (1 mL) freshly ground pepper
1 stalk celery with leaves, chopped
1 small onion, finely chopped
2 tbsp (30 mL) fresh parsley, chopped
1 ½ tsp (7 mL) fresh thyme, chopped or ½ tsp (2 mL) dried
1 tbsp (15 mL) fresh tarragon, chopped or 1 ½ tsp (7 mL) dried
1 tsp (5 mL) fresh rosemary, chopped or ¼ tsp (1 mL) dried
lemon wedges and fresh herbs

Rinse fish and pat dry. With sharp knife make 4 shallow diagonal slashes through skin on both sides. Brush cavity of fish with half the lemon juice and lightly spray with vegetable oil. Sprinkle cavity with pepper. Combine celery, onion, parsley, thyme, tarragon and rosemary; stuff fish with herb mixture and close with skewers. Brush outside of fish with remaining lemon juice and lightly spray with oil.

To barbecue, place fish on double thickness of foil, wrap and secure. Heat barbecue coals to medium-hot and place foil-wrapped fish on grill. Cook fish 10 to 12 minutes for each inch (2.5 cm) of thickness at the thickest part. Halfway through cooking, turn fish to cook on other side. To test for doneness, make a small slit in the foil and with a sharp knife carefully examine flesh. Fish is cooked when flesh flakes easily and has turned opaque.

To bake, preheat oven to 400°F (200°C). Place fish on well-oiled baking sheet, and allow 10 minutes for each inch (2.5 cm) of thickness. Carefully examine flesh with a sharp knife to test for doneness. Garnish whole salmon with lemon wedges and generous sprigs of fresh herbs.

Serves 8.

Nutrient Analysis per serving:	
Calories 327	Potassium 708mg
Calories from Fat 172 (53%)	Carbohydrates 4g
Total Fat 19g	Fibre 1g
Saturated Fat 4g	Sugar 1g
Cholesterol 100mg	Protein 34g
Sodium 114mg	

BARBECUED BREAST OF DUCK WITH COCONUT AND GRILLED VEGETABLES

Benmiller Inn, Goderich, ON

The Benmiller Inn features this duck dish cooked medium-rare so as not to toughen the succulent flesh. They baste it with a rich butter and mustard sauce which I have replaced with low-fat Beer Basting Sauce. Serve with Rhubarb Chutney (p. 148), a delicious accompaniment to duck, pork or chicken.

Duck and Vegetables

3 boneless, skinless duck breasts, each 8 oz (250 g)
1 bunch asparagus
1 medium eggplant
1 sweet red pepper
1 green pepper
1 small zucchini
1 red onion, cut into 8 sections
vegetable oil spray
2 tbsp (30 mL) toasted unsweetened coconut

Beer Basting Sauce

This sauce is also good with beef, pork and lamb.

½ (125 mL) cup beer
3 tbsp (45 mL) Dijon mustard
2 tbsp (30 mL) white wine vinegar
2 tbsp (30 mL) fresh lemon juice
grated zest of a lemon
1 tbsp (15 mL) olive oil
1 ½ tsp (7 mL) honey
1 clove garlic, minced
2 tbsp (30 mL) chopped fresh thyme or tarragon

For the duck and vegetables:

Cover duck breasts with ¼ cup (60 mL) Beer Basting Sauce and refrigerate 1 to 6 hours.

Prepare vegetables while barbecue grill is heating. Break off and discard tough ends of asparagus. Unless asparagus is very tender, use a vegetable peeler to remove skin from lower 2 in (5 cm) of stalks. Cut eggplant, peppers and zucchini into 1 ¼-in (3-cm) chunks and place in a glass pan along with asparagus. Toss with ¼ cup (60 mL) Beer Basting Sauce.

Place vegetables in a grilling basket over medium-high heat; cook, turning basket occasionally and basting regularly with Beer Basting Sauce, for about 10 minutes or until tender. Keep an eye on the asparagus as it tends to scorch.

Meanwhile, blot duck breasts with paper towels, spray with oil and place on grill. Cook for about 5 minutes per side or until medium-rare, basting regularly with sauce. Remove breasts from grill and let rest on a cutting board for 5 minutes.

Arrange grilled vegetables on a platter or on 6 individual plates. Carefully slice breasts into thin strips and arrange on top of vegetables. (At the Benmiller Inn they serve the sliced duck on a separate platter arranged in star shape.) Sprinkle with toasted coconut.

For the basting sauce:
Whisk together all ingredients in a small bowl. Use to marinate and baste meat and vegetables.

Serves 6.

Nutrient Analysis per serving:

Calories 223	Potassium 600mg
Calories from Fat 80 (36%)	Carbohydrates 11g
Total Fat 9g	Fibre 4g
Saturated Fat 3g	Sugar 5g
Cholesterol 86mg	Protein 25g
Sodium 164mg	

MOLASSES-AND-RUM-GLAZED SALMON

Who would have thought that Nova Scotian ingredients like molasses and rum would make a wonderful marinade for salmon? Try it on the barbecue, but watch carefully so it doesn't scorch.

6 skinless salmon fillet portions, each 4 oz (125 g)
½ cup (125 mL) orange juice
¼ cup (60 mL) dark rum
2 tbsp (30 mL) molasses
1 tbsp (15 mL) Dijon mustard
2 tsp (10 mL) Worcestershire sauce
freshly ground pepper

To make the marinade, combine all ingredients except salmon in a glass baking dish that is large enough to hold the fillets in a single layer. Immerse fillet pieces in marinade and refrigerate for up to 4 hours, turning once.

Remove salmon from marinade a few minutes before cooking and let rest on a platter. Grill on a preheated barbecue over medium heat.

If you prefer cooking inside, transfer salmon to a lightly oiled baking sheet and bake at 400°F (200°C) for about 10 minutes. Spoon about 1 tbsp (15 mL) of marinade over each portion and broil for a minute or so until it bubbles. Watch carefully so it doesn't burn.

Serves 6.

Nutrient Analysis per serving:	
Calories 261	Potassium 569mg
Calories from Fat 112 (43%)	Carbohydrates 8g
Total Fat 12g	Fibre 0g
Saturated Fat 2g	Sugar 5g
Cholesterol 67mg	Protein 23g
Sodium 117mg	

SEA SCALLOPS WITH WINE AND LEMON ON SKEWERS

Sea scallops bathed in a wine-citrus marinade team up with zucchini and small tomatoes to make a colourful succulent dish. This makes a lovely meal in the summer on the barbecue or you can stick them under the broiler. Sometimes, if we are in a hurry, we grill them in a mesh basket instead of on skewers. Serve with this versatile tartar sauce that you can flavour with minced garlic, chives, green onions or fresh dill. We like it with most fish dishes. When choosing a "light" mayonnaise, be sure to check nutrition labels for the product lowest in sodium and fat.

Scallops

1 ½ lb (750 g) large sea scallops
¼ cup (60 mL) dry white wine
1 tbsp (15 mL) fresh lemon or lime juice
1 tbsp (15 mL) olive oil
2 cloves garlic, minced
3 tbsp (45mL) chopped green onions
2 tbsp (30 mL) finely chopped parsley
¼ tsp (1 mL) freshly ground pepper
2 small zucchini cut in 1-in (2.5-cm) pieces
12 cherry tomatoes

Tartar Sauce

¼ cup (60 mL) light mayonnaise
⅓ cup (75 mL) fat-free plain yogurt
1 green onion, finely chopped
2 tbsp (30 mL) fresh dill chopped, optional
cayenne, optional

For the scallops:

Rinse scallops and remove tough muscle. Dry on paper towels. To prepare marinade, combine wine, lemon juice, olive oil, garlic, onions, parsley and pepper in a small bowl and pour into a sealable heavy plastic bag. Add scallops, remove most of the air from the bag and refrigerate for at least 30 minutes.

Heat barbecue to medium. Thread scallops and vegetables onto skewers starting and finishing with a cherry tomato and alternating scallops and zucchini pieces in between. (If using wooden skewers, soak them for an hour to prevent burning.) Reserve marinade for basting.

Barbecue for about 10 minutes or just until done, basting occasionally, and turning several times.

Serves 6.

Nutrient Analysis per serving:	
Calories 144	Potassium 623mg
Calories from Fat 31 (22%)	Carbohydrates 7g
Total Fat 3g	Fibre 1g
Saturated Fat 0g	Sugar 1g
Cholesterol 34mg	Protein 17g
Sodium 189mg	

For the tartar sauce:

Combine in a small bowl and season with cayenne, if desired.

Serves 6, 2 tbsp (30 mL) each.

Nutrient Analysis per serving:

Calories 31
Calories from Fat 18 (58%)
Total Fat 2g
Saturated Fat <1g
Cholesterol 3mg
Sodium 20mg

Potassium 38mg
Carbohydrates 3g
Fibre 0g
Sugar 0g
Protein 1g

GRILLED VEGETABLE AND HERBED RICOTTA NAPOLEON

The Holiday Inn, Lake Muskoka, ON

This very flavourful and healthy dish created by Executive Chef Steve Potts makes a great vegetarian entrée. Placing the marinated vegetables in a grilling basket makes it easier to cook them evenly and turn over without losing them through the grate.

Marinade

6 tbsp (90 mL) white wine
2 tbsp (30 mL) virgin olive oil
2 tbsp (30 mL) balsamic vinegar
1 large clove garlic, minced
2 tbsp (30 mL) chopped fresh basil
2 tbsp (30 mL) chopped fresh coriander
2 tbsp (30 mL) chopped fresh thyme
freshly ground pepper

Vegetables

6 Portobello mushrooms, stems removed
1 large sweet red pepper
1 large sweet yellow pepper
2 green zucchini
1 eggplant
1 large red onion
1 large tomato
vegetable oil spray
12 oz (375 g) ricotta cheese 4% milk fat
few drops of hot sauce
2 tbsp (30 mL) balsamic vinegar
6 cups (1.5 L) assorted baby lettuces
6 sprigs of basil or thyme

For the marinade:

To make the marinade, combine in a bowl wine, olive oil, vinegar, garlic and half of each of the basil, coriander and thyme, and pepper.

For the vegetables:

Place mushrooms in a glass pan. Cut peppers into slivers and zucchini and eggplant into slices, all ¼ in (6 mm) thick. Cut onion and tomato into 6 slices. Add these vegetables to mushrooms. Brush marinade over vegetables; cover and let stand for up to 1 hour.

Spray vegetables with oil and transfer to greased grill over high heat or under broiler on high, discarding marinade. Cook for about 5 minutes per side until tender, less for tomatoes. Remove and set aside.

Meanwhile, in bowl, combine ricotta cheese, remaining basil, coriander and thyme, and pepper to taste.

Spray baking sheet with oil. Divide vegetables evenly into 6 portions and stack them starting with eggplant and ending with Portobello mushroom, spreading ricotta mixture between some of the layers. Bake in 350°F (180°C) oven for 6 to 8 minutes.

Meanwhile place greens in centre of each of 6 plates and drizzle with balsamic vinegar. Top with grilled vegetable napoleon. Garnish with a fresh sprig of basil or thyme.

Serves 6.

Nutrient Analysis per serving:

Calories 226	Potassium 1506mg
Calories from Fat 69 (31%)	Carbohydrates 29g
Total Fat 8g	Fibre 9g
Saturated Fat 3g	Sugar 8g
Cholesterol 18mg	Protein 14g
Sodium 100mg	

SESAME-HALIBUT KEBABS WITH PINEAPPLE AND HONEY

The combo of halibut with juicy fresh pineapple, crisp zucchini and red pepper becomes something memorable when flavoured with lime, honey and fragrant seasoning. Asian five-spice powder with its overtones of anise and cinnamon gives a subtle flavour to the dish, but cumin or coriander can also be used. If you use wooden skewers, soak them at least an hour before using.

2 tbsp (30 mL) fresh lime juice
1 tbsp (15 mL) olive oil
1 tbsp (15 mL) liquid honey
1 tsp (5 mL) low-sodium soy sauce
1 clove garlic, minced
1 tsp (5 mL) five-spice powder
¼ tsp (1 mL) freshly ground black pepper
1 red pepper
2 small zucchini
½ fresh pineapple, peeled and cored
1 lb (500 g) skinless halibut
1 tbsp (15 mL) sesame seeds

In a large bowl, combine lime juice, olive oil, honey, soy sauce, garlic, five-spice powder and black pepper.

Cut red pepper, zucchini, pineapple and halibut into 1 ¼-in (3-cm) pieces and add to bowl, stirring to coat evenly.

Thread fish and vegetables onto skewers, alternating vegetables, fish and pineapple, beginning and ending with red pepper.

Barbecue over medium heat on a greased grill, turning once. Sprinkle with sesame seeds when fish is almost cooked. Kebabs can also be cooked in the oven under the broiler, cooking 2 to 3 minutes on each side.

Serves 4.

Nutrient Analysis per serving:	
Calories 223	Potassium 854mg
Calories from Fat 50 (23%)	Carbohydrates 18g
Total Fat 6g	Fibre 3g
Saturated Fat 1g	Sugar 13g
Cholesterol 36mg	Protein 26g
Sodium 82mg	

CHAMPAGNE-GLAZED ROCK CORNISH GAME HENS

Amherst Shore Country Inn, Lorneville, NS, and Blomidon Inn, Wolfville, NS

This blueberry-infused entrée is the creation of the chefs at the Amherst Shore Country Inn and Blomidon Inn. They also prepare the dish using eight quails, 4 oz (125 g) each. Cooking time for quails is approximately half the time allotted Cornish hens. The amount of glaze is sufficient to marinate 3 game hens.

2 Rock Cornish game hens, 1 lb (500 g) each
½ cup (125 mL) blueberries
1 cup (250 mL) orange juice
2 cloves garlic, minced
2 tbsp (30 mL) cider vinegar
2 tbsp (30 mL) champagne
1 tsp (5 mL) low-sodium soy sauce
½ tsp (2 mL) cinnamon
1 tbsp (15 mL) fresh tarragon, finely chopped
2 tsp (10 mL) fresh thyme, finely chopped
freshly ground black pepper
vegetable oil spray

Blueberry-Champagne Glaze
3 tbsp (45 mL) blueberry preserve
1 tbsp (15 mL) champagne
1 tsp (5 mL) low-sodium soy sauce
1 tsp (5 mL) olive oil

For the cornish hens:
Remove and discard skin, fat and wing tips from birds. Rinse and pat dry. Using kitchen shears, split hens in half lengthwise along centre of breastbone and back.

Purée blueberries in a blender with half the orange juice. Add remaining juice along with garlic, vinegar, champagne, soy sauce, cinnamon and herbs; season with pepper and pour over birds in a shallow dish. Turn to coat, cover with plastic wrap and marinate refrigerated 4 hours or overnight.

Preheat grill to medium using both burners. Discard marinade and pat birds dry with paper towels. Spray birds with vegetable oil and barbecue, turning once before turning over, to create a diamond pattern. Reduce heat and continue cooking until birds are almost done. Brush with Blueberry-Champagne Glaze and close the lid of the barbecue. Cook until tender. Brush with additional glaze and serve.

For the glaze:
Combine all ingredients and whisk to blend.

Serves 4.

Nutrient Analysis per serving:	
Calories 207	Potassium 377mg
Calories from Fat 46 (22%)	Carbohydrates 13g
Total Fat 5g	Fibre 1g
Saturated Fat 1g	Sugar 8g
Cholesterol 108mg	Protein 24g
Sodium 105mg	

SLOW & SAVOURY

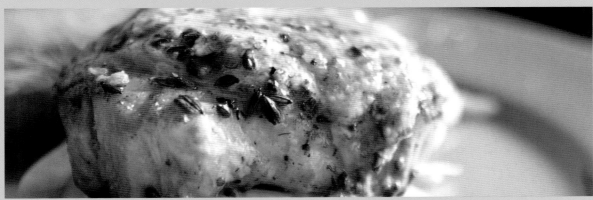

JACK'S GLORIOUS GOULASH

The Innlet Café, Mahone Bay, NS

Goulash, a Hungarian specialty, is a thick, highly spiced stew made from browned beef. Owner-chef Jack Sorenson perfected this recipe many years ago by using lean steak such as bottom sirloin, trimmed of all fat. Shank beef is also recommended because of its robust flavour. Jack used tamari sauce which I replaced with low-sodium soy sauce. For a variation to this glorious dish, add cooked small potatoes, carrots, onions and whole green beans to the sauce with the mushrooms and simmer for 30 minutes. Serve over cooked noodles. Garnish with poppy seeds.

1 ½ lb (750 g) lean beef steak
vegetable oil spray
2 medium onions, sliced
2 tsp (10 mL) paprika
2 cloves garlic, crushed
1 cup (250 mL) diced fresh tomatoes
1 tsp (5 mL) cider vinegar
1 cup (250 mL) water
½ cup (125 mL) dry red wine
¼ tsp (1 mL) freshly ground pepper
1/2 tsp (2 mL) caraway seeds, crushed
2 tbsp (30 mL) flour
¼ cup (60 mL) cold water
1 tbsp (15 mL) low-sodium soy sauce
¾ tsp (3 mL) dry marjoram
2 cups (500 mL) mushrooms, sliced

Cut beef into 1-in (2.5-cm) cubes and brown in a preheated heavy Dutch oven that has been well sprayed with vegetable oil. Add onions and continue to cook and stir until they become golden. If they stick to the bottom of the pan, add a bit of water. Sprinkle with paprika and continue cooking for a couple of minutes.

Add garlic, tomatoes, vinegar, water, wine, pepper and caraway seeds and bring to a boil. Reduce heat and simmer covered for 1 ½ hours, until meat is fork-tender.

Remove meat from saucepan and measure volume of liquid. Bring to 1 ⅓ cups (325 mL) by reducing or adding water. Whisk flour with cold water and stir into sauce. Simmer, stirring until thickened.

Add soy sauce, marjoram and mushrooms and simmer 5 minutes. Return meat to the sauce and bring to serving temperature.

Serves 4.

Nutrient Analysis per serving:	
Calories 297	Potassium 899mg
Calories from Fat 93 (31%)	Carbohydrates 12g
Total Fat 10g	Fibre 2g
Saturated Fat 3g	Sugar 4g
Cholesterol 73mg	Protein 39g
Sodium 140mg	

SWEDISH STYLE MEATLOAF

This low-fat meatloaf, rich with onions and allspice, is made with a combination of lean ground beef and chicken. Storing the cooked loaf in the refrigerator overnight allows the flavours to develop.

Swedish Style Meatloaf
1 cup (250 mL) fresh whole-wheat breadcrumbs
½ cup (125 mL) rolled oats
⅔ cup (150 mL) buttermilk
1 egg
1 cup (250 ml) coarsely chopped onions
2 large cloves garlic
½ tsp (2 mL) each freshly ground pepper and allspice
¼ tsp (1 mL) each nutmeg and ginger
1 tbsp (15 mL) low-sodium soy sauce
¼ cup (60 mL) chopped fresh dill
¾ lb (375 g) lean ground beef
¾ lb (375 g) ground chicken or turkey

Yogurt-Horseradish Sauce
1 cup (250 mL) fat-free yogurt
1 tbsp (15 mL) low-fat mayonnaise
2 tbsp (30 mL) prepared horseradish
2 tbsp (30 mL) chopped fresh dill

For the meatloaf:
Preheat oven to 425°F (220°C).

Place breadcrumbs and rolled oats in a large bowl and set aside.

Combine buttermilk, egg, onions and garlic in blender and process until puréed. Pour over breadcrumbs and rolled oats and mix in. Add spices, soy sauce, dill and ground meats and combine evenly.

Transfer meat to an oiled 9x5-in (23x12-cm) loaf pan and bake at 425°F (220°C) for 15 minutes. Reduce heat to 350°F (180°C) and continue baking for 45 minutes longer or until meatloaf shrinks away from the side of the pan and is cooked in the centre. Remove from oven and let stand for a while. Cut into 8 slices.

Serve with Yogurt-Horseradish Sauce.

Serves 8.

Nutrient Analysis per serving:

Calories 285	Potassium 278mg
Calories from Fat 115 (40%)	Carbohydrates 17g
Total Fat 12g	Fibre 2g
Saturated Fat 4g	Sugar 2g
Cholesterol 70mg	Protein 25g
Sodium 150mg	

For the horseradish sauce:
Whisk together yogurt, mayonnaise and horseradish. Stir in dill.

Nutrient Analysis per serving:

Calories 11	Potassium 34mg
Calories from Fat 4 (37%)	Carbohydrates 1g
Total Fat <1g	Fibre 0g
Saturated Fat 0g	Sugar 0g
Cholesterol 1mg	Protein 1g
Sodium 21mg	

DAN HATFIELD'S BEEF AND BEER OVEN STEW

My son-in-law, Dan Hatfield, in Fredericton, has developed this wonderful aromatic and savoury stew that he makes with the local Picaroon's Best Bitter (dark beer but not as dark as stout). The flavour of this easy-to-make dish that is baked in the oven improves upon standing, so make it one day and serve the next.

1 lb (500 g) stewing beef
3 tbsp (45 mL) whole-wheat flour
4 small onions, cut in half
2 large carrots, cut in chunks
2 medium parsnips, diced
2 stalks celery, cut in chunks
3 medium potatoes, cut in chunks
1 ⅓ cups (325 mL) diced turnip
2 large cloves garlic, minced
6 mushrooms, cut in half
1 cup (250 mL) dark beer
1 ⅓ cups (325 mL) water
3 tbsp (45 mL) tomato paste
1 tbsp (15 mL) low-sodium soy sauce
2 tsp (10 mL) Worcestershire sauce
1 bay leaf
1 tsp (5 mL) dried thyme
½ tsp (2 mL) dried oregano
¼ cup (60 mL) chopped parsley, optional

Trim all fat from beef and cut into 1-in (2.5-cm) cubes. Spread flour on a piece of waxed paper and dredge beef in it. Transfer beef to a large Dutch oven and reserve flour.

Add onions, carrots, parsnips, celery, potatoes, turnip, garlic and mushrooms. Combine beer, water, tomato paste, soy sauce and Worcestershire sauce in a bowl and whisk in reserved flour. Pour over vegetables. Add bay leaf, thyme and oregano and stir to mix.

Place over medium heat and cook for 10 minutes, stirring occasionally while oven heats to 325°F (160°C). Transfer to oven and bake for about 2 ½ hours or until meat is very tender. Sprinkle with chopped parsley, if desired, and serve from the Dutch oven.

Serves 6.

Nutrient Analysis per serving:	
Calories 304	Potassium 1429mg
Calories from Fat 45 (15 %)	Carbohydrates 44g
Total Fat 5g	Fibre 8g
Saturated Fat 1g	Sugar 11g
Cholesterol 33mg	Protein 22g
Sodium 173mg	

ROASTED PORK LOIN WITH PRUNE AND APPLE

10
2 hrs

Gowrie House Country Inn, Sydney Mines, NS

Clifford Matthews of Gowrie House Country Inn has created a wonderful dish that is simple to prepare but will wow your guests with its excellent flavour and attractive presentation. He broiled the meat for about 25 minutes before roasting it, but I tried an alternate method, roasting it at 450°F (230°C) for 10 minutes, then reducing heat to 350°F (180°C) for about 2 hours.

½ tsp (2 mL) each of allspice, ground bay leaves and thyme
2 ½ lb (1.25 kg) lean pork loin, deboned and tied
16 pitted prunes
1 cup (250 mL) water
½ cup (125 mL) dry white wine
3 Granny Smith apples
2 tbsp (30 mL) maple syrup
½ tsp (2 mL) allspice (2nd amount)
vegetable oil spray

Mix together allspice, bay leaves and thyme. (Grind bay leaves in a coffee grinder.) Rub pork with spices, place in a plastic bag and refrigerate for several hours. Remove pork from the refrigerator and allow it to come to room temperature before roasting.

Meanwhile, prepare prune and apple garnish. Add prunes, water and wine to a saucepan and simmer until prunes are plumped. Strain and reserve the prune juice. Set prunes aside. Peel, core and section the apples into eighths. Place them in an oiled baking dish and drizzle maple syrup over top. Sprinkle with half the allspice and spray lightly with vegetable oil. Set aside to cook with loin.

Preheat oven to 450°F (230°C). Roast the pork for 10 minutes, then reduce heat to 350°F (180°C) and continue cooking 1 ½ to 2 hours or until the internal temperature of the meat reaches 150°F (66°C). While pork is roasting, place the dish of apples on centre rack of oven and bake 30 to 40 minutes until apples are browned and soft. Turn the apples over after 25 minutes and sprinkle with remaining allspice. Reserve meat on a warm platter, cover lightly with foil.

Remove any fat from the pan and add the reserved prune juice to the pan juices; deglaze the pan over medium-high heat. Warm the prunes in a microwave oven, approximately 30 seconds on high.

Serve pork, thinly sliced, garnished with prunes and apple segments with drizzled pan juices over all.

Serves 8.

Nutrient Analysis per serving:	
Calories 302	Potassium 784mg
Calories from Fat 86 (29%)	Carbohydrates 20g
Total Fat 10g	Fibre 2g
Saturated Fat 3g	Sugar 14g
Cholesterol 78mg	Protein 32g
Sodium 66mg	

ORIENTAL OVEN-FRIED PORK CHOPS WITH GINGER AND GARLIC

This is an easy way to prepare mouth-watering pork chops. Ginger, garlic, sherry and soy sauce give an exotic flavour to crumb-coated chops that become crisp and brown while baking. Pop a few potatoes and pieces of squash in the oven to bake with them for an easy dinner. Serve with Old-Fashioned Applesauce (p. 128).

1 beaten egg
2 tbsp (30 mL) low-sodium soy sauce
1 tbsp (15 mL) dry sherry
⅛ tsp (½ mL) powdered ginger
 or ½ tsp (2 mL) minced fresh ginger
½ tsp (2 mL) garlic powder or 1 clove garlic, minced
freshly ground pepper
4 tbsp (60 mL) fine dry breadcrumbs
4 lean boneless centre rib pork chops, each 4 oz (125 g)

Combine egg, soy sauce, sherry, ginger, garlic and pepper in a pie plate.

Spread crumbs on a piece of waxed paper. Dip chops in egg mixture, then roll in crumbs and place on a greased baking sheet.

Bake at 350°F (180°C) for 30 minutes. Turn them over and bake about 20 minutes longer until tender and showing no pink.

Serves 4.

Nutrient Analysis per serving:	
Calories 206	Potassium 500mg
Calories from Fat 72 (35%)	Carbohydrates 5g
Total Fat 8g	Fibre <1g
Saturated Fat 3g	Sugar 1g
Cholesterol 76mg	Protein 26g
Sodium 123mg	

PORK CHOPS DIJONNAISE WITH FENNEL

This dish is fine enough to serve to company, but easy enough for everyday. Fennel seeds give these chops braised with wine and Dijon mustard a mellow licorice flavour. Add more wine and mustard, if you like. Serve with Old-Fashioned Applesauce (p.128).

4 thick lean pork chops, each 5 oz (140 g) bone-in
1 tbsp (15 mL) crushed fennel seeds
½ tsp (2 mL) freshly ground pepper
1 tsp (5 mL) olive oil
4 tsp (20 mL) smooth or grainy Dijon mustard
1 clove garlic, crushed
½ tsp (2 mL) dry thyme
½ cup (125 mL) dry red wine

Press crushed fennel and pepper into the chops. Brown them in oil in a heavy oven-proof skillet.

Spread each chop with 1 tsp (5 mL) mustard and sprinkle with garlic and thyme. Add wine and simmer, covered, until tender — about 40 minutes. Turn chops at least once during cooking. Wine sauce should be thick when chops are done. Cook uncovered for a few minutes to thicken, if necessary.

To serve, spoon sauce over chops.

Serves 4.

Nutrient Analysis per serving:	
Calories 258	Potassium 669mg
Calories from Fat 97 (38%)	Carbohydrates 2g
Total Fat 11g	Fibre 1g
Saturated Fat 3g	Sugar 0g
Cholesterol 78mg	Protein 32g
Sodium 130mg	

MADRAS VEGETABLE CURRY

This mild, creamy curry makes a fine vegetarian entrée or side dish. Add cayenne or jalapeño pepper if you prefer a spicier taste. This is a versatile curry and you can add other vegetables such as carrots, mushrooms, yellow summer squash or tomatoes. I have made it with low-fat coconut milk which creates a creamy sauce, but you can use water instead. Just add a little more tomato paste to thicken the sauce. Serve with Steamed Brown Rice (p. 143).

2 tsp (10 mL) olive oil

1 large onion, chopped

3 cloves garlic, minced

1 tbsp (15 mL) fresh ginger, minced

1 tbsp (15 mL) mild curry paste

1 tbsp (15 mL) curry powder

1 ½ cups (375 mL) low-fat coconut milk

¾ cup (175 mL) water

2 red potatoes, diced

1 sweet potato, peeled and diced

3 cups (750 mL) cauliflower flowerets

1 small zucchini, cut in chunks

2 ½ cups (625 mL) green beans, broken in half

1 cup (250 mL) peas

½ cup (125 mL) raisins or currants

3 tbsp (45 mL) tomato paste

fresh coriander, chopped

Heat oil in Dutch oven and sauté onion until soft. Add garlic and ginger and cook for a minute. Stir in curry paste and curry powder and continue cooking for a minute. Add coconut milk and water, followed by sweet potato, cauliflower, zucchini, beans, peas and raisins. Stir well to coat vegetables.

Bring to a boil, cover and simmer for 10 minutes, stirring occasionally. Add more water if vegetables seem dry. Continue cooking for 10 minutes or until all vegetables are tender. Stir in tomato paste and simmer uncovered a few minutes longer.

Scatter coriander over top and serve.

Serves 10, 1 cup (250 mL) each.

Nutrient Analysis per serving:	
Calories 134	Potassium 606mg
Calories from Fat 31 (23%)	Carbohydrates 24g
Total Fat 3g	Fibre 4g
Saturated Fat 2g	Sugar 9g
Cholesterol 0mg	Protein 4g
Sodium 80mg	

COQ AU VIN WITH TOMATO AND BRAISED GREENS

The Amphora Tapas Bar at Hainle Vineyards Estate Winery, Peachland, BC

Coq au vin is a traditional French fricassee of rooster or chicken and wine that legend traces to ancient Gaul and Julius Caesar. Chef David Forestell has created a savoury version using crushed tomatoes and a variety of herbs and spices that takes comfort food to a new level. He includes star anise, a licorice-flavoured ingredient of Chinese five-spice powder, found in Asian food stores and some supermarkets. I used skinless, bone-in chicken thighs which worked well. Serve the dish over a bed of noodles.

1 tbsp (15 mL) oil
2 lb (1 kg) boneless, skinless chicken pieces (thighs, breasts) trimmed of fat
8 small shallots or pearl onions, peeled
1 onion, diced
1 tbsp (15 mL) liquid honey
1 tsp (5 mL) coarsely ground pepper
14 oz (398 ml) crushed Italian plum tomatoes, no salt added
1 cup (250 mL) water
½ bottle (375 mL) Pinot Noir or other red wine
8 or more whole mushrooms
2 bay leaves
2 sprigs savory or ¼ tsp (1 mL) dried
3 juniper berries or allspice berries
1 whole clove
2 star anise
2-in (5-cm) cinnamon stick
¼ orange, cut in 2 wedges
½ lb (250 g) fall greens (kale, rhubarb chard, mustard or beet in combination), washed and coarsely chopped

Heat oil in a large heavy Dutch oven and brown chicken in batches over medium-high heat. Remove and set aside. Sauté shallots and onions over medium-high heat for 3 to 5 minutes, or until beginning to brown. Add honey and pepper; cook for about 15 minutes over medium heat until onions are caramelized. Remove from pan and add to chicken.

Add tomatoes and water to pan and cook over medium-high heat, stirring occasionally, until liquid is reduced to about half of its volume. Add wine to pan along with reserved chicken, onions and mushrooms; bring to boil. Add bay leaves, savory, juniper berries, clove, star anise, cinnamon stick and orange wedges. Remove from heat.

Cover and bake in a 350°F (180°C) oven for 1 ½ hours or until liquid is reduced and thickened sufficiently to add "shine" to chicken. (Dish can be prepared to this point up to 24 hours in advance, covered and refrigerated; reheat n oven.)

About 15 minutes before serving, poke greens into liquid around chicken and return pan to oven. Before serving, remove bay leaves, star anise, cinnamon stick and orange segments.

Serves 6.

Nutrient Analysis per serving:	
Calories 246	Potassium 719mg
Calories from Fat 48(19%)	Carbohydrates 13g
Total Fat 5g	Fibre 3g
Saturated Fat 1g	Sugar 6g
Cholesterol 105mg	Protein 27
Sodium 249mg	

ROASTED LOIN OF PORK WITH GOLDEN HARVEST SAUCE

The Old Orchard Inn, Greenwich, NS

Crispy roast pork makes a fine meal, especially complemented with this delicious sauce created by Chef Joe Gillis. When buying pork, be aware that many fresh pork cuts are now labeled as "seasoned" which means they have been soaked in brine to tenderize them. Avoid these as they have a high sodium content.

2 ½ lb (1.25 kg) lean loin of pork, boneless and rolled
1 clove garlic, halved
vegetable oil spray
freshly ground black pepper
¾ cup (175 mL) diced pumpkin
¼ cup (60 mL) diced sweet potato
¾ cup (175 mL) diced squash
½ carrot, peeled and chopped
½ onion, peeled and chopped
1 clove garlic, chopped
½ apple, peeled and chopped
1 cup (250 mL) water
1-in (2.5-cm) cinnamon stick
1 tsp (5 mL) curry powder, or to taste
1 ½ tsp (7 mL) honey or maple syrup
1 small bay leaf
freshly ground pepper, to taste
1 ½ tbsp (22 mL) fresh lemon juice, or to taste
fresh sage or chives

Preheat oven to 450°F (230°C).

Rinse pork loin and pat dry; rub with garlic halves, spray lightly with vegetable oil and season liberally with pepper. Roast 10 minutes then reduce heat to 350°F (180°C) and continue to roast, allowing 30 minutes per pound or until the internal temperature of the meat reaches 160°F (70°C). Remove from oven, tent with foil and let rest for 10 minutes before slicing.

While pork is roasting, prepare sauce. Bring remaining ingredients except pepper, lemon juice and sage to a boil in a large saucepan over medium-high heat. Reduce heat and simmer, stirring occasionally, until vegetables are fully cooked, about 30 minutes. Discard cinnamon stick and bay leaf and purée sauce in a blender. Season to taste with pepper and lemon juice, and keep warm.

To serve, arrange pork slices on plates and top with golden harvest sauce. Garnish with chopped fresh sage or chives.

Serves 8.

Nutrient Analysis per serving:

Calories 248	Potassium 734mg
Calories from Fat 86 (35%)	Carbohydrates 8g
Total Fat 9g	Fibre 2g
Saturated Fat 3g	Sugar 3g
Cholesterol 78mg	Protein 32g
Sodium 72mg	

SLOW-COOKED ROAST BEEF WITH WINE GRAVY

Pot roasting is perfect for less tender cuts of beef and slow cooking allows development of rich beefy flavour. Choose a lean cut of beef such as sirloin tip.

2 ½ lb (1.25 kg) roast of beef
olive oil spray
½ tsp (2 mL) freshly ground pepper
½ cup (125 mL) red wine
1 cup (250 mL) water
2 tsp (10 mL) Dijon mustard
½ tsp (2 mL) Worcestershire sauce
2 cloves garlic, crushed
2 tbsp (30 mL) instant flour

Rinse roast with cold water and pat dry. Heat a heavy skillet and spray with oil. Sear all sides of the roast over medium-high heat. Transfer meat to a slow cooker and sprinkle with pepper.

In a small bowl whisk together wine, ¾ cup (175 mL) water, mustard and Worcestershire sauce. Pour over beef. Add garlic.

Cover and cook on high for 5 hours or on low for 8 hours or until fork-tender. Remove beef from pot and cover with a tent of foil.

To make gravy add remaining ¼ cup (60 mL) water to the cooker and scrape brown bits from the sides and bottom. Transfer to a medium bowl and skim off fat. Whisk in instant flour and cook in a microwave until thickened and bubbling, stirring several times.

Slice the beef and serve with gravy.

Serves 8.

Nutrient Analysis per serving:

Calories 224	Potassium 499mg
Calories from Fat 78 (35%)	Carbohydrates 2g
Total Fat 8g	Fibre 0g
Saturated Fat 2g	Sugar 0g
Cholesterol 61mg	Protein 30g
Sodium 97mg	

BRUNCH OR
INFORMAL DINNERS

CORNMEAL-CRUSTED SALMON CAKES WITH APRICOT AND CURRANT CHUTNEY

Windsor House, St Andrews-by-the-Sea, NB

Chef Peter Woodworth has created exotically seasoned salmon cakes that not only have excellent flavour, but also are versatile. They make an elegant brunch dish, accompanied by Apricot and Currant Chutney, but we also enjoy them in an informal setting served on whole-wheat buns topped with lettuce, onion, tomato, Dijon mustard and Yogurt and Caper Dressing (p. 149). Apricot and Currant Chutney is also delicious with roast pork.

Salmon Cakes
1 lb (500 g) fresh salmon fillet, cut in several pieces
4 tbsp (60 mL) chopped green onions
1 clove garlic, minced
2 egg whites
¼ tsp (1 mL) freshly ground pepper
4 tbsp (60 mL) soft breadcrumbs
⅔ cup (150 mL) cornmeal
1 tbsp (15 mL) cumin
1 tsp (5 mL) cayenne pepper
½ tsp (2 mL) cinnamon
2 tbsp (30 mL) finely chopped fresh tarragon
4 tsp (20 mL) olive oil

Apricot and Currant Chutney
1 cup (250 mL) diced sun-dried apricots
⅔ cup (150 mL) chopped sweet onion or shallots
2 cloves garlic, minced
1 cup (250 mL) white wine
½ cup (125 mL) water
1 tbsp (15 mL) honey
½ cup (125 mL) white wine vinegar or cider vinegar
¼ cup (60 mL) dried currants
2 tbsp (30 mL) sliced almonds

For serving
crisp greens
steamed asparagus
whole-wheat burger buns
lettuce
sliced tomato and onion
Dijon mustard

For the salmon:
Combine salmon, green onions, garlic, egg whites, pepper and breadcrumbs in a food processor. Pulse a few times until salmon is coarsely chopped.

Rinse your hands with cold water and form the salmon mixture into 6 patties. Refrigerate several hours or overnight to help keep shape when cooking.

On a piece of waxed paper, combine cornmeal, cumin, cayenne, cinnamon and tarragon. Gently press into the patties.

Place a non-stick pan over medium heat, add olive oil and transfer patties to the pan with a spatula. Sauté until golden brown, turning very carefully only once.

Serves 6.

Nutrient Analysis per serving:
Calories 202	Potassium 352mg
Calories from Fat 105 (52%)	Carbohydrates 6g
Total Fat 12g	Fibre 1g
Saturated Fat 2g	Sugar 0g
Cholesterol 45mg	Protein 17g
Sodium 80mg	

For the chutney:

Combine all ingredients in a heavy saucepan and place over medium-high heat. Bring to a boil, then simmer on medium heat for about 12 minutes or until thickened, stirring occasionally. Let cool.

Makes about 2 cups (500 mL), 10 servings of 3 tbsp (45 mL) each.

For serving:

Serve salmon cakes with crisp greens, steamed asparagus and Apricot and Currant Chutney.

Serve on whole-wheat burger buns with lettuce, sliced tomato and onion, Dijon mustard and Yogurt and Caper Dressing.

Nutrient Analysis per serving:	
Calories 68	Potassium 270mg
Calories from Fat 0	Carbohydrates 14g
Total Fat 0g	Fibre <1g
Saturated Fat 0g	Sugar 2g
Cholesterol 0mg	Protein 1g
Sodium 4mg	

THAI CRAB CAKES

Raincoast Café, Tofino, BC

Café owner Lisa Henderson has developed a delightful fishcake, combining crab meat and white fish with crunchy fresh bean sprouts and tangy Thai flavours with hints of cilantro and hot pepper. Serve with Apricot and Currant Chutney (p. 75) or Tartar Sauce (p. 49).

2 lb (1 kg) cooked halibut, haddock or cod, flaked
1 lb (500 g) crab meat
1 ¼ cups (310 mL) panko or slightly dry breadcrumbs
1 cup (250 mL) fresh bean sprouts, coarsely chopped
¼ cup (60 mL) finely chopped green onions
⅓ cup (75 mL) finely chopped fresh cilantro
2 tbsp (30 mL) fresh lime juice
⅛ tsp (½ mL) red pepper flakes
1 tsp (5 mL) oyster sauce
1 large egg
2 egg whites
¼ cup (60 mL) whole-wheat flour
½ tsp (2 mL) paprika
1 tbsp (15 mL) olive oil

Combine fish, crab, breadcrumbs, bean sprouts, green onions, cilantro, lime juice, red pepper flakes and oyster sauce in a large mixing bowl. Slightly beat egg and egg whites and add to crab mixture, mixing well. With wet hands, form into 12 patties and refrigerate for several hours.

Coat chilled crab cakes with mixture of whole-wheat flour and paprika. Add half the olive oil to a non-stick skillet that has been placed over medium-high heat. Sauté half the crab cakes until golden brown on both sides, turning once. Repeat with remaining crab cakes.

Serves 12, one 4 oz (125 g) crab cake each.

Nutrient Analysis per serving:

Calories 166	Potassium 523mg
Calories from Fat 38 (23%)	Carbohydrates 5g
Total Fat 4g	Fibre 1g
Saturated Fat 1g	Sugar 1g
Cholesterol 80mg	Protein 26g
Sodium 209mg	

BISTRO-STYLE SALMON WITH HONEY-MUSTARD SAUCE

Elaine Elliot and Virginia Lee

You can quickly whip up this tasty dish and serve it either hot or cold. Any leftover sauce will keep, refrigerated, for a week and is great on sandwiches.

Bistro-style salmon
6 salmon steaks, 4 oz (125 g) each
1 cup (250 mL) dry white wine
½ cup (125 mL) water
¼ cup (60 mL) green onions or shallots, minced

Honey-Mustard Sauce
⅓ cup (75 mL) Dijon mustard
⅓ cup (75 mL) plain yogurt
1 ½ tbsp (22mL) liquid honey
3 tbsp (45 mL) fresh dill, minced or 2 tsp (10 mL) dried dill
2 tbsp (30 mL) fresh lemon juice

For the salmon:
Preheat oven to 400°F (200°C). Place salmon steaks in a large baking dish and add wine and water. Sprinkle with green onions. Bake, uncovered, basting often with wine mixture until fish is light pink and done to taste, approximately 12 to 15 minutes. Transfer salmon to individual warmed plates. Serve with Honey-Mustard Sauce.

For the sauce:
Combine all ingredients in a small bowl and whisk until smooth. Serve over salmon.

Refrigerate remaining sauce. Makes approximately 1 cup (250 mL).

Serves 6.

Nutrient Analysis per serving:	
Calories 213	Potassium 418mg
Calories from Fat 99 (46%)	Carbohydrates 7g
Total Fat 11g	Fibre 0g
Saturated Fat 2g	Sugar 5g
Cholesterol 57mg	Protein 20g
Sodium 234mg	

BLACKENED FISH SOFT TACOS

Serve this spicy fish with cool, crunchy Tangy Rainbow Slaw (p.144) wrapped up in a corn tortilla. Corn tortillas have much less salt than most flour tortillas. The Tartar Sauce (p. 49) and Tangy Slaw can be made in advance as they will keep for several days in the refrigerator.

Blackened Fish Soft Tacos

1 lb (500 g) haddock fillets, or other white fish
½ tbsp (7 mL) olive oil
8 6-in (15-cm) corn tortillas
1 sliced avocado
1 large diced tomato

Spice Mix

4 tsp (20 mL) paprika
1 tsp (5 mL) each garlic powder and onion powder
1 tsp (5 mL) freshly ground black pepper
1 tsp (5 mL) each dried oregano and thyme
½ tsp (2mL) cayenne, optional

Prepare Spice Mix, Tartar Sauce and Tangy Rainbow Slaw; set aside.

Rinse fish, drain on paper towels and cut into 8 portions. Spread Spice Mix on a piece of waxed paper and roll fish pieces in it to coat.

Heat a non-stick pan and add olive oil. Sauté fish over medium-high heat until the surface is darkened and fish flakes when tested with a fork.

Heat tortillas briefly one at a time in a dry skillet until hot and softened. Cover with a paper towel.

To assemble tacos, layer some slaw, avocado and a piece of fish on each tortilla. Spoon on a dollop of Tartar Sauce and top with diced tomato. Fold over and serve. Serve extra slaw on the side.

Serves 4, 2 tacos each.

Nutrient Analysis per serving:	
Calories 283	Potassium 754mg
Calories from Fat 91 (32%)	Carbohydrates 24g
Total Fat 11g	Fibre 7g
Saturated Fat 2g	Sugar 1g
Cholesterol 65mg	Protein 25g
Sodium 100mg	

HADDOCK WITH ALMOND PUFF TOPPING

This is an excellent dish with great taste and presentation, plus it is easy to prepare.

12 oz (375 g) haddock fillet
1 tbsp (15 mL) lemon juice
1 tsp (5 mL) Dijon mustard
freshly ground pepper
1 large egg white
1 ½ tbsp (22 mL) low-fat mayonnaise
3 tbsp (45 mL) chopped or sliced toasted almonds

Cut haddock into 3 portions. Combine lemon juice and mustard in a small bowl and spread over fish. Season with pepper.

Place in an oiled baking dish and bake at 450°F (230°C) for 10 minutes per inch of thickness or until fish flakes easily when pierced with a fork.

Beat egg white until stiff. Fold in mayonnaise and spread on cooked fish. Top with toasted almonds. Return to the oven for 3 minutes to brown. Place briefly under broiler, if necessary.

Serves 3.

Nutrient Analysis per serving:	
Calories 181	Potassium 444mg
Calories from Fat 68 (38%)	Carbohydrates 3g
Total Fat 8g	Fibre 1g
Saturated Fat 1g	Sugar 1g
Cholesterol 67mg	Protein 25g
Sodium 179mg	

JESSIE'S CURRIED CHICKPEAS

My friend, Jessie Macdonald, brought this yummy dish to one of our potluck dinners and it was a big hit. It makes a fine vegetarian main course when served with Steamed Brown Rice (p. 143) and a green salad. If you have time, cook the chickpeas from scratch. Soak 1 ¼ cups (310 mL) dried chickpeas with enough water to cover overnight and then bring them to a boil and simmer covered for about 1 ½ hours or until tender. When time is short, I use brands of canned chickpeas that are lower in salt than most.

½ tbsp (7 mL) olive oil
1 tsp (5 mL) mustard seeds
1 sweet green pepper, coarsely chopped
1 onion, chopped
2 or 3 cloves garlic, crushed
1 tsp (5 mL) finely chopped fresh ginger
2 tsp (10 mL) curry powder
½ tsp (2 mL) turmeric
½ tsp (2 mL) ground coriander
¼ tsp (1 mL) pepper
1 tsp (5 mL) Worcestershire sauce
1 28-oz (796 mL) can salt-free diced tomatoes
2 tbsp (30 mL) flaked coconut
2 cups (500 mL) cooked chickpeas
1 tbsp (15 mL) lemon juice
1 tsp (5 mL) honey
2 tbsp (30 mL) chopped fresh basil

Heat oil and add mustard seeds in a heavy pan or Dutch oven. Cover and shake over medium heat until the seeds pop. Add green pepper, onion, garlic and ginger and cook until onion is transparent.

Stir in curry, turmeric, coriander, pepper and Worcestershire sauce and continue cooking for a few minutes. Add tomatoes and coconut. Simmer uncovered over low heat for 30 minutes.

Add chickpeas, lemon juice and honey and cook covered for 20 minutes longer. Stir in chopped basil shortly before serving. Garnish with basil.

Serves 6.

Nutrient Analysis per serving:

Calories 140	Potassium 563mg
Calories from Fat 28 (20%)	Carbohydrates 24g
Total Fat 3g	Fibre 5g
Saturated Fat 1g	Sugar 7g
Cholesterol 0mg	Protein 6g
Sodium 154mg	

WHISTLER CRAB CAKES

Rim Rock Café, Whistler, BC

Chef Rolf Gunther sparks the flavour of his crab cakes with red, green, yellow and jalapeño peppers. This makes a fine luncheon dish served on mixed greens. Chef makes a dramatic presentation by placing one cake on top of another, wrapping a long slice of cucumber marinated in Japanese rice wine around the edges, and topping them with shredded daikon radish and orange flying fish roe. Serve with Tzatziki (p. 140).

1 lb (500 g) cooked crab meat, drained
⅓ cup (75 mL) finely diced red pepper
⅓ cup (75 mL) finely diced green pepper
⅓ cup (75 mL) finely diced yellow pepper
¼ cup (60 mL) finely minced jalapeños
¼ cup (60 mL) finely minced shallots or sweet onion
3 egg whites, lightly beaten
2 tsp (10 mL) puréed roasted garlic*
1 cup (250 mL) fresh breadcrumbs
freshly ground pepper, to taste
1 tbsp (15 mL) olive oil

* Roasted garlic has a more mellow flavour than raw garlic, with a smooth, buttery texture. To roast, drizzle head of garlic with olive oil, wrap in foil and roast in 350°F (180°C) oven until very soft. Makes an excellent spread.

Combine crab meat, peppers, onion, egg whites, roasted garlic, breadcrumbs and ground pepper. Rinse hands with cold water and form crab mixture into patties. Refrigerate at least 1 hour.

Pan fry in hot olive oil in a non-stick skillet until golden brown on both sides.

Serves 8, one 4 oz (125 g) crab cake each.

Nutrient Analysis per serving:

Calories 120	Potassium 325mg
Calories from Fat 23 (19%)	Carbohydrates 8g
Total Fat 3g	Fibre 1g
Saturated Fat <1g	Sugar 1g
Cholesterol 43mg	Protein 15g
Sodium 236mg	

VEGGIE CHIPOTLE QUESADILLAS

A quesadilla is a savoury Mexican turnover made with a flour or corn tortilla, stuffed with cheese and served hot. This low-fat version is plump with tender vegetables and seasoned with hot chipotle peppers (smoked jalapeños), which are available dried, or canned in adobo sauce, at most grocery stores. When buying tortillas be sure to check the nutritional content as some brands are high in sodium.

2 tsp (10 mL) olive oil
1 large onion, chopped
½ large red pepper, chopped
6 mushrooms, chopped
1 clove garlic, minced
½ cup (125 mL) cooked corn kernels
2 cups (500 mL) cooked small broccoli florets
1 cup (250 mL) cold skimmed milk
3 tbsp (45 mL) flour
1 chipotle pepper, finely chopped
¼ cup (60 mL) grated low-fat old cheddar
¼ cup (60 mL) chopped cilantro
4 whole grain tortillas, 6-in (15-cm) diameter
chopped tomatoes and fat-free yogurt

Heat oil in a skillet and sauté onion until translucent. Add red pepper, mushrooms and garlic, continuing to cook until vegetables are tender. Stir in corn and broccoli and set aside.

Whisk flour into skimmed milk in a small saucepan. Cook over medium heat while stirring often until thickened. about 6 minutes. Stir in chipotle pepper and cheese. Pour over vegetables in skillet and evenly combine. Sprinkle with cilantro.

Spread about ¼ of the filling on half a tortilla and fold it over, making a quesadilla. Place on a baking sheet. Repeat with remaining tortillas.

Bake at 425°F (220°C) for 5 to 8 minutes or until hot and bubbling. Serve at once with bowls of chopped tomatoes and fat-free plain yogurt.

Serves 4.

Nutrient Analysis per serving:	
Calories 219	Potassium 541mg
Calories from Fat 45 (20%)	Carbohydrates 37g
Total Fat 5g	Fibre 4g
Saturated Fat 1g	Sugar 8g
Cholesterol 2mg	Protein 10g
Sodium 249mg	

DRESSED-UP BAKED FISH

This family favourite can be prepared in minutes with the help of a microwave oven. Any kind of fish fillets or steaks such as haddock, halibut or salmon can be used. Savoury stuffing on top of the fish keeps it moist during cooking. I never measure crumbs and lemon juice but go by taste and texture; the amounts below are just a guide.

1 tbsp (15 mL) olive oil
¼ cup (60 mL) chopped green onion
½ cup (125 mL) finely chopped celery
½ cup (125 mL) chopped mushrooms
½ cup (125 mL) soft breadcrumbs, torn by hand or prepared in a food processor
1 tbsp (15 mL) lemon juice
¼ cup (60 mL) 2% milk
freshly ground pepper
4 pieces of haddock fillet, each 4 oz (125 g)
parsley or dill for garnish

Combine oil and vegetables and microwave in a heat-proof bowl on high for 3 minutes, or until tender. Stir in breadcrumbs, lemon juice, milk and pepper to make a spreadable stuffing. Add more crumbs or milk to get desired consistency.

Arrange fish pieces in a shallow heat-proof pan. Divide stuffing among the 4 pieces of fish and spread evenly over top.

Cover pan with plastic wrap and microwave on high for 5 or 6 minutes or until fish flakes when tested with a fork. Garnish with fresh parsley or dill.

Serves 4.

Nutrient Analysis per serving	
Calories 170	Potassium 467mg
Calories from Fat 55 (32%)	Carbohydrates 5g
Total Fat 6g	Fibre 1g
Saturated Fat 2g	Sugar 1g
Cholesterol 70mg	Protein 23g
Sodium 135mg	

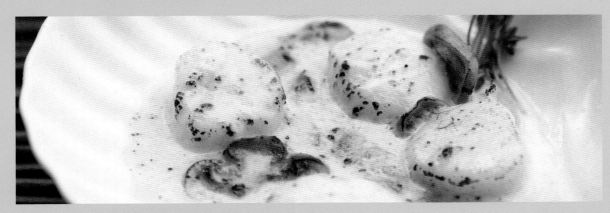

SIMPLY ELEGANT
DINNERS

COQUILLES ST. JACQUES

This dish is quite simple to make and will impress friends and family, especially if served in real scallop shells or "coquilles." Use a good white wine such as an Australian Chardonnay for a tasty sauce. Serve with baked potato, puréed carrots and whole green beans.

Scallops

½ cup (125 mL) dry white wine

½ cup (125 mL) water

2 tbsp (30 mL) green onions or shallots

freshly ground pepper

pinch of fresh thyme

1 small bay leaf

1 lb (500 g) scallops

½ tbsp (7 mL) olive oil

8 oz (250 g) fresh mushrooms, sliced

2 ½ tbsp (37 mL) freshly grated Parmesan cheese

Sauce

1 ½ tbsp (22 mL) soft olive oil margarine

4 tbsp (60 mL) flour

wine broth

¾ cup (175 mL) skimmed milk

¼ cup (60 mL) blend 10% cream

1 tbsp (15 mL) Parmesan cheese

For the scallops:

Combine wine, water, green onions, pepper, thyme and bay leaf in a saucepan and simmer for 5 minutes. Rinse and drain scallops and cut large ones in half. Add to pan and simmer for a few minutes just until cooked. Drain scallops and transfer to a bowl. Discard the bay leaf and reserve broth for the sauce.

Heat olive oil in a frying pan and sauté mushrooms for about 5 minutes or until their juice is absorbed. Add to scallops.

For the sauce:

Put margarine in a medium-sized bowl and melt in the microwave. Stir in flour and cook for about 2 minutes or until it bubbles. Whisk in the wine broth drained from the scallops and the milk as well as 1 tbsp Parmesan cheese. Microwave for 3 minutes or longer until the sauce bubbles and thickens. Stir with a whisk several times.

Add scallops and mushrooms to sauce and stir in a few tablespoons of milk if sauce is too thick. Spoon into scallop shells or small ramekins. Sprinkle with remaining Parmesan cheese.

Bake at 400°F (200°C) for 10 minutes or until the tops start to brown. Broil for a minute or so, if desired.

Serves 6.

Nutrient Analysis per serving:	
Calories 183	Potassium 495mg
Calories from Fat 63 (34%)	Carbohydrates 10g
Total Fat 7g	Fibre 1g
Saturated Fat 2g	Sugar 1g
Cholesterol 30mg	Protein 15g
Sodium 217mg	

CAJUN SPICED SALMON WITH
TOMATO SALSA AND ROASTED SEAWEED

Dalvay-by-the-Sea, PEI

This tasty and attractive dish is a fusion of southern Cajun spices and the sea tang of Japanese roasted nori seaweed, which can be found in most Asian markets or specialty food stores. Serve it with jasmine rice, steamed asparagus and Tomato Salsa (p. 146).

Cajun Salmon
4 fillets of salmon or salmon steaks, 5 oz (140 g) portions
¼ to ½ cup (60 to 125 mL) Cajun Spice Mix*
1 tbsp (15 mL) vegetable oil
1 sheet roasted nori seaweed, cut into thin strips with scissors

Cajun Spice Mix
2 tbsp (30 mL) paprika
2 tbsp (30 mL) garlic powder
1 tbsp (15 mL) black pepper
1 tbsp (15 mL) crushed red pepper flakes
1 tbsp (15 mL) dried thyme
1 tbsp (15 mL) dried oregano
1 tbsp (15 mL) onion powder
½ tbsp (7 mL) ground white pepper
1 tsp (5 mL) dry mustard powder

* Cajun Spice Mix can be purchased but usually contains much salt, so make your own to reduce sodium.

For the salmon:
Dredge salmon fillets in Cajun Spice Mix on a sheet of waxed paper. Heat a heavy skillet until very hot and smoking. Put salmon fillets in dry pan and add enough oil to moisten fish. Pan may flame so be careful. Quickly turn salmon to sear other side. Remove skillet from heat and place in a preheated 400°F (200°C) oven. Cook for approximately 5 to 7 minutes or until fish flakes and is opaque, being careful not to overcook.

To serve, place salmon on warmed plates and surround each fillet with Tomato Salsa (p. 146). Scatter shredded seaweed over top of each fillet.

Serves 4.

For the spice mix:
Mix all ingredients in a glass jar. Seal tightly and store in a cool, dry place.

Makes about ½ cup (125 mL).

Nutrient Analysis per serving:

Calories 334	Potassium 710mg
Calories from Fat 176 (53%)	Carbohydrates 10g
Total Fat 20g	Fibre 3g
Saturated Fat 4g	Sugar 2g
Cholesterol 84mg	Protein 3g
Sodium 88mg	

CHICKEN BREAST CHARLOTTE LANE

Charlotte Lane Café and Crafts, Shelburne, NS

Chef Roland Glauser has married cranberries, fresh orange, ginger and honey in an elegant sauce that complements spicy baked chicken. This dish is easy to prepare but classy enough for a dinner party.

Chicken

2 tsp (10 mL) curry powder
½ tsp (2 mL) paprika
1 tsp (5 mL) ground rosemary
dash freshly ground black pepper
4 skinless, boneless chicken breasts, each 4 oz (125 g)
vegetable oil spray

Sauce

¾ cup (175 mL) fresh orange juice
1 tbsp (15 mL) fresh ginger, grated
3 tbsp (45 mL) honey
1 cup (250 mL) cranberries
2 tsp (10 mL) cornstarch
1 tbsp (15 mL) cold water
1 large orange, peeled, pith removed and sectioned

For the chicken:

Preheat oven to 350°F (175°C). Combine curry, paprika, rosemary and pepper on a piece of waxed paper. Dredge chicken breasts in seasoning and arrange in a shallow baking dish. Spray breasts lightly with vegetable oil and bake in oven for 20 to 30 minutes until done.

For the sauce:

Combine orange juice, ginger, honey and cranberries in a small saucepan and bring to a boil. Reduce heat and simmer until cranberries are soft but not mushy. Combine cornstarch and water and stir in enough to create a slightly thickened sauce. Add orange segments and heat through.

To serve, pour sauce over chicken breasts.

Serves 4.

Nutrient Analysis per serving:	
Calories 237	Potassium 501mg
Calories from Fat 19 (8%)	Carbohydrates 28g
Total Fat 2g	Fibre 3g
Saturated Fat <1g	Sugar 21g
Cholesterol 66mg	Protein 27g
Sodium 77mg	

PECAN-CRUSTED TROUT WITH ORANGE-WHISKY SAUCE

La Perla, Dartmouth, NS

Chef James MacDougall makes his whisky sauce with bourbon that he flames after adding it to the reduced orange juice to burn off the alcohol. When I tried this, it scorched the side of the saucepan so I omitted the flaming and the alcohol cooked off during the reduction. Chef serves his spectacular entrée with saffron rice pilaf and fresh green beans.

Pecan-crusted trout

1 16 oz (500 g) trout fillet
¼ cup (60 mL) whole-wheat flour
¼ tsp (1 mL) salt-free lemon pepper
⅓ cup (75 mL) chopped pecans
1 ½ tbsp (22 mL) dry breadcrumbs
2 egg whites, beaten with a whisk
½ tbsp (7 mL) each olive oil and olive oil margarine
Orange-Whisky Sauce
orange slices, for garnish

Orange-Whisky Sauce

⅔ cup (150 mL) fresh orange juice
⅓ cup (75 mL) bourbon or Canadian rye whisky
½ tsp (2 mL) instant flour

For the trout:

Preheat oven to 350°F (180°C). Rinse and pat dry the trout fillet and cut into 4 equal portions. Dredge pieces in flour, shaking off excess, and season with lemon pepper. Combine pecans and breadcrumbs on a piece of waxed paper. Brush the fillets with egg white and crust with pecan crumb mixture. Heat oil and margarine in a pan over medium-high heat and fry fish, flesh side down for about 30 seconds and then turn fillets over. Finish the trout in oven, for about 8 minutes, depending upon the thickness of the fillets. Serve drizzled with Orange-Whisky Sauce and garnish with orange slices.

Serves 4.

For the sauce:

In a small saucepan, heat orange juice over high heat; reduce volume by half. Remove saucepan from heat, add bourbon and carefully ignite to burn off the alcohol. Whisk in instant flour. Return pan to heat and cook until sauce is reduced by half again.

Makes ½ cup (125 ml), 2 tbsp (30 mL) per serving.

Nutrient Analysis per serving:	
Calories 191	Potassium 196mg
Calories from Fat 89 (46%)	Carbohydrates 10g
Total Fat 10g	Fibre g
Saturated Fat 1g	Sugar 4g
Cholesterol 4mg	
Sodium 62mg	

MARY JANE'S MALAYSIAN LOBSTER CURRY

*My friend Mary Jane Covert wowed our Gourmet Group
with this lobster curry made with coconut milk and a variety
of spices. She accompanied it with sambals, or condiments,
such as bananas cut into fingers and fresh or canned
mandarin orange segments sprinkled with a little coconut.
Serve with Steamed Brown Rice (p. 143).*

2 cups (500 mL) finely chopped onions

2 cloves garlic, minced

2 tsp (10 mL) olive oil

2 tsp (10 mL) finely minced fresh ginger

½ tsp (2 mL) ground cumin

1 tsp (5 mL) ground coriander

2 tbsp (30 mL) ground almonds

¼ tsp (1 mL) dried chili pepper flakes, optional

1 tsp (5 mL) turmeric

1 tsp (5 mL) Patak's mild curry paste

2 cups (500 mL) diced fresh tomatoes

1 tbsp (15 mL) cornstarch

1 tbsp (15 mL) cold water

2 cups (500 mL) light coconut milk

1 lb (500 g) cooked lobster meat cut in pieces

2 tsp (10 mL) finely chopped capers

2 cups (500 mL) English cucumber, seeded and cut into
   ½-in (1.2-cm) dice

1 tbsp (15 mL) fresh lime juice

3 tbsp (45 mL) chopped fresh cilantro

Sauté onions and garlic in oil in a Dutch oven until soft. Add
ginger, cumin, coriander, almonds, chili peppers, turmeric
and curry paste and stir fry for 2 minutes. Add tomatoes and
bring to a boil. Cover and cook over low heat for 5 minutes.

Mix cornstarch with water and add to coconut milk. Gradually
stir into the tomato mixture. Cook and stir until thickened.

Add lobster and cook over low heat for 10 minutes. Stir in
capers, cucumbers and lime juice and continue cooking for 5
minutes. Garnish with chopped cilantro.

Serves 8, ¾ cup (175 mL) each.

Nutrient Analysis per serving:	
Calories 151	Potassium 57 mg
Calories from Fat 46 (31%)	Carbohydrate 12g
Total Fat 5g	Fibre 2g
Saturated Fat 3g	Sugar 4g
Cholesterol 41mg	Protein 14g
Sodium 258mg	

PAN-SEARED BREAST OF CHICKEN WITH BRAISED RUBY CHARD AND RHUBARB WINE

Kettle Creek Inn, Port Stanley, ON

Executive Chef Frank Hubert uses rhubarb wine from a local winery, Quai Du Vin, to add subtle flavour to this colourful combination of ruby chard and chicken. I used a dry pink zinfandel and a mixture of ruby, golden and green chard combined with green onions and garlic to make this dish.

6 boneless chicken breast pieces, each 4 oz (125 g)
1 tbsp (15 mL) chopped fresh rosemary
paprika
freshly ground black pepper
1 tbsp (15 mL) extra-virgin olive oil
large bunch of ruby chard or Swiss chard, about 1 lb (500 g)
2 green onions, chopped
2 cloves garlic, thinly sliced
1 ⅛ (280 mL) cups rhubarb wine
2 tbsp (30 mL) chopped shallots or green onions
¼ tsp (1 mL) crushed black peppercorns
½ tbsp (7 mL) soft olive oil margarine

Sprinkle chicken with rosemary and dust lightly with paprika and pepper. In a large non-stick oven-proof skillet, heat oil over medium-high heat; sear chicken until golden brown but not cooked through. Remove from pan and set aside.

Wash, dry and shred chard, cutting stems into 1-in (2.5-cm) pieces on the bias. Discard any tough stems.

Reheat the pan used for the chicken and add green onions, garlic and chard stems. Sauté over medium heat for about 5 minutes. Add chard and about half of the wine. Bring to a boil, reduce heat and simmer for 5 minutes or until chard is almost tender.

Arrange chicken pieces on top of the chard and cover the pan. Roast at 400°F (200°C) for about 10 minutes or until chicken is no longer pink inside. Transfer chicken and chard to a platter and keep warm.

Place pan over medium-high heat and add remaining wine and shallots. Boil until reduced by half. Whisk in peppercorns and margarine. Remove from heat.

Divide chard among 6 plates and place chicken on top. Drizzle sauce over the chicken and serve.

Serves 6.

Nutrient Analysis per serving:	
Calories 193	Potassium 560 mg
Calories from Fat 34 (18%)	Carbohydrates 4 g
Total Fat 4g	Fibre 1 g
Saturated Fat 1g	Sugar 1 g
Cholesterol 66mg	Protein 27g
Sodium 180mg	

TURKEY DIVAN

Some cooks make Turkey or Chicken Divan with canned cream of mushroom soup, mayonnaise and sour cream, but you can have an excellent Divan without all those high-fat ingredients. This delicious recipe combines leftover turkey, broccoli and 2 cheeses in a white wine sauce. My tasters couldn't believe that this dish was low in sodium and fat. Be sure to remove as much moisture as possible from cooked broccoli so it won't make the sauce runny.

12 oz (375 g) cooked turkey breast
1 tbsp (15 mL) dry sherry
1 lb (500 g) broccoli
2 ½ tbsp (37 mL) cornstarch
1 cup (250 mL) 1% milk
1 bay leaf
¼ cup (60 mL) dry white wine
1 tbsp (15 mL) finely chopped green onion or chives
½ cup (125 mL) grated low-fat old cheddar cheese
⅓ cup (75 mL) freshly grated Parmesan cheese
cayenne
freshly grated nutmeg, to taste
1 tbsp (15 mL) dry breadcrumbs
chopped parsley for garnish

Preheat oven to 400°F (200°C). Slice turkey breast about ¼ in (6 mm) thick and arrange in an oiled 8-in (20-cm) baking pan. Sprinkle with sherry.

Cut broccoli lengthwise into thin slices and boil until tender. Drain well and blot on paper towels to remove as much moisture as possible. Arrange over turkey.

Whisk cornstarch into some of the milk in a large glass measuring cup or bowl; then stir in remaining milk and bay leaf. Microwave for 2 minutes. Add wine and green onion and microwave for about 3 minutes or until thick and bubbling, stirring several times. Remove bay leaf.

Stir in cheddar and Parmesan cheese and season with cayenne and nutmeg. Pour sauce evenly over broccoli. Sprinkle breadcrumbs on top.

Bake at 400°F (200°C) for 10 to 12 minutes or until bubbling. Put under broiler to lightly brown the top, if desired.

Serves 4.

Nutrient Analysis per serving	
Calories 232	Potassium 716mg
Calories from Fat 24 (10%)	Carbohydrate 15g
Total Fat 3g	Fibre <1g
Saturated Fat 1g	Sugar 3g
Cholesterol 77mg	Protein 34g
Sodium 189mg	

CHICKEN VERONIQUE

Loon Bay Lodge, St. Stephen, NB

Veronique refers to a dish garnished with grapes. This elegant and easy entrée uses sweet, juicy green grapes which are a perfect complement to wine-infused chicken, delicately seasoned with nutmeg and fresh tarragon. As a bonus, this dish is low in sodium and high in potassium.

4 chicken breasts, boneless and skinless, each 4 oz (125 g)
½ cup (125 mL) crumbs from low-salt soda crackers
¼ tsp (1 mL) freshly ground black pepper
1 ½ tsp (7 mL) chopped fresh tarragon or ½ tsp (2 mL) dried
pinch freshly grated nutmeg
4 tsp (20 mL) olive oil
¼ cup (60 mL) chopped onion
2 cups (500 mL) sliced mushrooms
½ cup (125 mL) water
½ cup (125 mL) white wine
2 cups (500 mL) seedless green grapes
sprigs of fresh tarragon for garnish

Place chicken breasts between 2 pieces of plastic wrap and pound to about ⅓ in (8 mm) thickness. Combine crumbs, pepper, tarragon and nutmeg on a sheet of waxed paper. Dredge chicken in crumb mixture. Heat oil in a large non-stick skillet and brown chicken on both sides. Transfer to a shallow baking dish.

Add onion and mushrooms to skillet and sauté until tender. Deglaze pan with water and wine. Pour over chicken and bake, uncovered at 375°F (190°C) for 20 to 25 minutes.

Add grapes to chicken and continue to bake until chicken is no longer pink in the centre, approximately 5 minutes. Serve garnished with fresh tarragon.

Serves 4.

Nutrient Analysis per serving	
Calories 298	Potassium 609mg
Calories from Fat 64 (22%)	Carbohydrates 15g
Total Fat 7g	Fibre 2g
Saturated Fat 1g	Sugar 14g
Cholesterol 66mg	Protein 29g
Sodium 134mg	

PASTA

CHICKEN AND ARTICHOKE PASTA WITH ALMONDS

I made up this low-fat recipe one night when I was in a hurry to prepare a quick family dinner, but it is fancy enough to serve at a dinner party. You can prepare the sauce in the time it takes to cook pasta and have everything ready in 20 minutes. For variety, add chopped fresh tomato or halved grape tomatoes after the sauce is cooked. This dish makes great leftovers. Serve with a crisp green salad.

16 oz (500 g) linguine
1 tbsp (15 mL) olive oil
1 lb (500 g) boneless, chicken breasts cut into 1-in (2.5-cm) cubes
1 onion cut into ¼-in (6-mm) dice
1 red pepper cut into ¼-in (6-mm) dice
2 cloves garlic, minced
½ tsp (2 mL) each dried thyme, oregano and basil
1 14-oz (398-mL) can no-salt-added tomato sauce
3 tbsp (45 mL) red wine
2 tbsp (30 mL) water
1 cup (250 mL) marinated artichoke hearts, rinsed, drained and
    coarsely chopped
freshly ground black pepper, to taste
½ tsp (2 mL) dry chili flakes, optional
½ cup (125 mL) almond slivers
½ cup (125 mL) or more chopped parsley
2 tbsp (30 mL) freshly grated Parmesan cheese

Cook linguine in a large pot of unsalted boiling water according to package instructions.

While linguine is cooking, heat oil in a large skillet and sauté chicken until it begins to brown. Add onion, pepper and garlic and continue to cook until softened. Stir in herbs.

Add tomato sauce, wine, water and artichoke hearts. Season with black pepper and chili flakes. Reduce heat to low and simmer uncovered for 5 minutes. Add a little water if sauce is too thick.

While sauce is cooking, toast slivered almonds at 350°F (180°C) until golden, about 7 minutes.

To serve, drain linguine when it is cooked al dente and transfer to a warmed pasta serving bowl. Pour chicken sauce over top and toss sauce with the pasta. Add parsley and toss again. Sprinkle Parmesan cheese and almonds over top.

Serves 8, about 2 cups (500 mL) each

Nutrient Analysis per serving:	
Calories 291	Potassium 493 mg
Calories from Fat 53 (18%)	Carbohydrate 47g
Total Fat 6g	Fibre 5g
Saturated Fat 1g	Sugar 4g
Cholesterol 6mg	Protein 12g
Sodium 57mg	

SINGAPORE NOODLES

The first time I had Singapore Noodles was at the China Classic restaurant in Halifax, one of the best Chinese restaurants in the city. The dish had a flavour that I couldn't identify which I subsequently learned came from Szechwan pepper. Native to Szechwan province in China, it is not actually a member of the pepper family but is the dried berry of a tree in the rue family. The berry is made up of an outer husk and inner black seed. It is the husk that is used for seasoning, first roasted to release aromatics, then ground in a coffee grinder. The flavour is peppery and slightly numbing to the lips and tongue.

6 oz (170 g) rice vermicelli noodles ⅛ in (3 mm) wide
4 dry shitake mushrooms
1 tbsp (15 mL) oil
8 oz (250 mg) boneless, skinless chicken breast,
    cut in ½-in (1.2-cm) strips
2 tsp (10 mL) finely minced fresh ginger
1 sweet red pepper, cut in thin slivers
1 medium carrot, peeled and cut in julienne strips
4 green onions, cut in 1-in (2.5-cm) pieces on the diagonal
½ cup (125 mL) thinly sliced sweet onion
½ cup (125 mL) celery, julienned
4 oz (125 g) snow peas, slivered
1 tsp (5 mL) finely minced fresh garlic
2 cups (500 mL) thinly sliced Napa cabbage, optional
½ cup (125 mL) Golden Vegetable Broth (p.115)
1 tbsp (15 mL) low-sodium soy sauce
2 tsp (10 mL) mild curry paste
1 ½ tsp (7 mL) sesame oil
2 tbsp (30 mL) fresh lime juice, optional
1 ½ cups (375 mL) fresh bean sprouts
8 oz (250 g) cooked salad shrimp
½ tsp (2 mL) ground Szechwan pepper or hot chili flakes
black sesame seeds for garnish

Pour boiling water over noodles and let stand for about 8 minutes or until softened. Drain well and set aside.

Soak shitake mushrooms in hot water until softened, about 10 minutes. Drain well, remove and discard tough stems. Slice mushrooms into thin strips.

Heat wok and add ½ tbsp (7 mL) oil. Sauté chicken and ginger until lightly browned. Remove and set aside. Add remaining ½ tbsp (7mL) oil to the wok and sauté pepper, carrot, onions, celery, snow peas and garlic for 2 minutes. Add Napa cabbage, and sauté for a minute longer.

Prepare sauce by combining broth, soy sauce, curry paste, sesame oil and lime juice. Add to the wok, cover and cook for a couple of minutes until vegetables are crisp tender.

Stir in bean sprouts, shrimp, chicken and noodles. Cook and stir gently until warmed through. Season with Szechwan pepper or chili flakes. To serve, sprinkle with black sesame seeds. For extra zip, sprinkle lightly with more ground Szechwan pepper.

Serves 8, 1 cup (250 mL) each.

Nutrient Analysis per serving:

Calories 212	Potasium 325mg
Calories from Fat 44 (21%)	Carbohycrates 27g
Total Fat 5g	Fibre 3g
Saturated Fat 1g	Sugar 3g
Cholesterol 60mg	Protein 15g
Sodium 173mg	

RICHARD'S FOUR-TASTE LINGUINE

My brother-in-law, Richard Gonzalez, is a super cook and pasta is one of his specialties. He claims he got this simple, tasty dish for garlic lovers from Luciano Pavarotti. I have added grilled scallops and recommend making it with Catelli Smart Linguine, which is white pasta with more fibre and better texture than most whole-wheat varieties. The sweetness of the scallops offers a foil to the bite of garlic and chili pepper. For variety, replace scallops with shrimp and add fresh lemon juice and zest.

½ lb (250 g) linguine
3 cloves garlic, finely minced
1 ½ tbsp (22 mL) olive oil
¾ lb (375 g) fresh scallops
paprika
3 tbsp (45 mL) tomato paste
½ tsp (2 mL) hot red chili pepper flakes
¾ cup (175 mL) chopped parsley
½ cup (125 mL) freshly grated Parmesan cheese, lightly packed
freshly ground pepper
a few parsley leaves for garnish

Cook linguine to al dente stage according to package instructions. Drain pasta and reserve about 1 cup (250 mL) of the cooking water.

While pasta is cooking, combine garlic and olive oil. Lightly brush scallops with garlic oil and sprinkle with paprika. Place a heavy skillet over high heat and sear scallops quickly on both sides to give a nice caramelized surface. Set aside and keep warm.

Combine remaining garlic oil, tomato paste and red pepper flakes to make the sauce. Mixture will be very thick and is not cooked. Add sauce to hot linguine and stir well. Mix in parsley and half of the Parmesan cheese. Stir in some reserved cooking water if the linguine is too dry. Season with pepper to taste.

Transfer linguine to a large warm bowl and sprinkle with remaining cheese. Arrange scallops on top and garnish with a bit of parsley leaf.

Serves 4, about 1 ¼ cups (310 mL) each.

Nutrient Analysis per serving:	
Calories 350	Potassium 591mg
Calories from Fat 69 (20%)	Carbohydrates 50g
Total Fat 8g	Fibre 7g
Saturated Fat 1g	Sugar 3g
Cholesterol 28mg	Protein 22g
Sodium 203mg	

KUSHARI

Kushari is a popular traditional dish in Egypt where many restaurants serve it exclusively. It is normally a vegetarian or vegan dish consisting of rice, lentils and pasta topped with a spicy tomato sauce and caramelized onions. Sometimes chickpeas are included and grilled meat is used as an additional topping. My version uses orzo, a rice-shaped pasta, rather than the traditional macaroni. Leftovers can be frozen and enjoyed as a side dish.

Rice

½ cup (125 mL) brown basmati rice
1 cup (250 mL) water
¼ cup (60 mL) finely chopped onion
1 clove garlic, minced

Lentils

½ cup (125 mL) small black lentils
1 ½ cups (375 mL) water
1 clove garlic, minced

Orzo

4 cups (1 L) water
¾ cup (175 mL) orzo
1 bay leaf

Hot Tomato Sauce

4 cups (1 L) coarsely chopped fresh tomatoes
3 cloves garlic, minced
½ tsp (2 mL) dried chili pepper seeds
1 tbsp (15 mL) red wine vinegar
1 tsp (5 mL) chopped capers

Carmelized Onions

½ tbsp (7 mL) olive oil
2 cups (500 mL) thinly sliced onions
½ tsp (2 mL) balsamic vinegar
freshly ground pepper

Rinse and drain rice. Combine with water, onion and garlic in a small covered saucepan and bring to a boil. Reduce heat and simmer for 35 to 40 minutes until tender.

Rinse and drain lentils. Combine with water and garlic in a small saucepan. Bring to a boil, cover and simmer for about 15 minutes, until tender. Be careful not to overcook as you don't want them broken and mushy. Drain off any remaining water.

To prepare the orzo, bring water to a boil and add orzo and bay leaf. Boil uncovered for about 10 minutes until it reaches the al dente state. Drain and set aside.

While the rice, lentils and orzo are cooking, prepare the tomato sauce. Combine tomatoes, garlic, chili pepper seeds and vinegar in a heavy saucepan. Bring to a boil, then reduce heat and simmer for about 25 minutes until thickened, stirring to break up tomatoes. Stir in capers.

To caramelize onions, place a non frying pan over high heat until very hot. Add oil and onions and stir-fry until onions begin to brown. Reduce heat and add vinegar and pepper, continuing to cook until onions are nicely browned.

To assemble kushari, mound the cooked rice, lentils and orzo in 3 adjacent piles on a large plate or platter. Top with dollops of hot tomato sauce and scatter caramelized onions on top. Pour remaining sauce into a bowl and serve at the table. An alternative way of serving is to combine rice, lentils and orzo with some of the tomato sauce and form into mounds.

Serves 6 generously.

Nutrient Analysis per serving

Calories 211	Potassium 573mg
Calories from Fat 18 (9%)	Carbohydrates 40g
Total Fat 2g	Fibre 8g
Saturated Fat 0g	Sugar 7g
Cholesterol 0mg	Protein 9g
Sodium 32mg	

SICILIAN PASTA

Marshlands Inn, Sackville, NB

This robust dish filled with fresh vegetables and seasoned with garlic and basil makes a satisfying vegetarian dinner. At the famous Marshlands Inn they serve it over colourful spinach fettuccini. To increase fibre, try it with whole-grain pasta.

1 medium red onion
6 medium tomatoes
8 oz (250 g) fresh mushrooms
¼ lb (125 g) snow peas
1 tbsp (15 mL) olive oil
6 cloves garlic, finely minced
3 or 4 tbsp (45 or 60 mL) chopped fresh basil
freshly ground pepper, to taste
1 cup (250 mL) water or vegetable stock
2 tbsp (30 mL) tomato paste
1 lb (500 g) spinach fettucine, cooked al dente
⅔ cup (150 mL) freshly grated Parmesan cheese
fresh basil leaves for garnish

Prepare vegetables by cutting onion and tomatoes into 1-in (2.5-cm) dice. Slice mushrooms and cut snow peas into slivers or 1-in (2.5-cm) pieces.

Heat oil in a large skillet over medium heat and sauté onion for a few minutes until golden. Add tomatoes, mushrooms, snow peas, garlic and basil and cook until vegetables soften. Season with pepper. Add water and tomato paste and bring to a boil.

Toss with hot pasta. Add ⅓ cup (75 mL) Parmesan cheese and toss again.

Serve garnished with remaining cheese and basil.

Serves 9, 1 ½ cups (375 mL)

Nutrient Analysis per serving	
Calories 392	Potassium 510mg
Calories from Fat 62 (16%)	Carbohydrate 66g
Total Fat 7g	Fibre 4g
Saturated Fat 2g	Sugar 4g
Cholesterol 10mg	Protein 17g
Sodium 188mg	

SOUPS

FRESH PEA SOUP WITH SHRIMP AND MINT

Beach Side Café, West Vancouver, BC

This sweet pea soup from Executive Chef Carol Chow is an all-season recipe as you can use fresh garden peas in the summer and rely on tender frozen peas at other times. Chef Chow served her soup chilled and garnished with crème fraiche. My variation is flavoured with mint and lime and topped with a dollop of yogurt. It is delicious served hot or cold.

½ tbsp (7 mL) soft olive oil margarine
½ yellow onion, diced
½ large leek (white part only) or 2 large green onions thinly sliced
1 stalk celery, chopped
1 or 2 cloves garlic, minced
2 ½ cups (625 mL) Golden Vegetable Broth (p. 115) or water
2 ½ cups (625 mL) fresh or frozen green peas
1 to 2 tbsp (15 to 30 mL) chopped fresh mint
zest from ½ lime
1 tsp (5 mL) fresh lime juice
freshly ground black pepper to taste
3 tbsp (45 mL) fat-free plain yogurt
3 oz (90 g) cooked shrimp, peeled and deveined
5 fresh mint leaves

Heat margarine over medium heat in a large saucepan; sauté onion, leek, celery and garlic for about 7 minutes. Add broth and peas; bring to boil. Reduce heat, cover and simmer for 5 minutes or until vegetables are tender. Remove pan from heat and set in a cold-water pan to cool.

Add mint, lime zest and juice to soup and purée in a blender in several batches until smooth. Season with pepper and more lime juice, if desired.

Refrigerate until chilled if serving cold, or reheat over medium-low heat to desired temperature, stirring occasionally.

Ladle into bowls and garnish with a dollop of yogurt, shrimp and a mint leaf.

Serves 5, 1 cup (250 mL) each

Nutrient Analysis per serving

Calories 107
Calories from Fat 17 (16%)
Total Fat 2g
Saturated Fat 1g
Cholesterol 34mg
Sodium 75mg
Potassium 339mg
Carbohydrates 15g
Fibre 5g
Sugar 5g
Protein 9g

SPICY DAHL

Red lentils and exotic seasonings make this hot Indian soup outstanding. We like it for lunch and I usually double the recipe as it doesn't last long. The hotness of jalapeño peppers can vary so add a bit to the soup and taste it before adding more.

Spicy Dahl

1 cup (250 mL) red lentils, rinsed
4 cups (1 L) water
3-in (7.5-cm) piece cinnamon stick
1 or 2 bay leaves
½ tsp (2 mL) turmeric
1 clove garlic, chopped
chopped cilantro

Seasoning Blend

1 tbsp (15 mL) oil
½ tsp (2 mL) mustard seeds
1 tsp (5 mL) cumin seeds
½ tsp (2 mL) or more mild curry paste
1 jalapeño pepper, finely chopped
1 cup (250 mL) finely chopped onion
1 tbsp (15 mL) pressed garlic
2 tsp (5 mL) fresh grated ginger
freshly ground pepper, to taste
1 tbsp (15 mL) low-sodium soy sauce

For the dahl:

Combine all ingredients, bring to a boil and simmer uncovered for 30 minutes. Blend until smooth. A hand-held immersible blender is ideal for this.

While lentils are cooking, prepare seasoning blend. Add to lentils and simmer for 15 minutes. Serve topped with a dollop of thick yogurt and chopped cilantro.

Serves 5, 1 cup (250 mL) each

For the seasoning:

Add oil and mustard seeds to a skillet and place over medium heat. Cover pan, shaking occasionally until seeds pop. Add cumin seeds and stir for a couple of minutes. Add remaining ingredients and stir-fry for 5 minutes. Stir seasoning blend into the soup and simmer as indicated.

Makes 6 servings of ¾ cup (175 mL) each.

Nutrient Analysis per serving

Calories 155	Potassium 5 mg
Calories from Fat 30 (19%)	Carbohydrate 24g
Total Fat 3g	Fibre 5g
Saturated Fat <1g	Sugar 1g
Cholesterol 0mg	Protein 9g
Sodium 44mg	

GOLDEN VEGETABLE BROTH

It is often difficult to find a low-sodium stock or broth to use in soups or sauces so I have developed this homemade version, which is tasty and has a golden colour. Design your broth according to what vegetables you have available and how flavourful a broth you want. Vegetables such as tomatoes, mushroom stems and shredded cabbage can be used in addition to those listed. The vegetables can be prepared in several ways. The simplest method is just to put all the veggies in a large pot and add water. If you want a richer flavour, first sauté them for about 10 minutes in a little oil to caramelize the sugars. For the most robust flavour, toss the vegetables with a little oil and roast them at 450°F (230°C) for 30 to 40 minutes before adding to the pot. The vegetable residue left after straining off the broth can be discarded but I like to purée it, freeze it in small quantities and add it to other soups. If you plan to do this, be sure to tie up the bay leaves, peppercorns and allspice berries in a small piece of cheesecloth so they can be easily removed.

2 large onions, peeled
2 large potatoes, unpeeled
1 sweet potato
1 parsnip
4 celery stalks
4 large carrots
1 medium zucchini
¼ rutabaga
light green stalks of 2 leeks
4 cloves garlic

6 dry shitake mushrooms
1 tbsp (15 mL) olive oil
½ tsp (2 mL) ground turmeric
3 bay leaves
½ tsp (2 mL) each black peppercorns and whole allspice
fresh chives, sprigs of thyme or tarragon
10 cups (2.5 L) water
1 tbsp (15 mL) low-sodium soy sauce

Prepare vegetables by chopping them coarsely. Add oil to a large heavy pot and place over medium-high heat. Transfer vegetables to the pot and cook, stirring often until they begin to turn golden.

Add remaining ingredients and bring to a boil. Cover and reduce heat; simmer for about 1 hour.

Set aside to cool slightly. Strain broth through a sieve or colander, pressing down on vegetables to squeeze out as much broth as possible. Adjust volume to 10 cups. Refrigerate or freeze broth in convenient amounts.

Makes 10 cups (2.5 L).

Nutrient Analysis per cup (250 mL):	
Calories 129	Sodium 79mg
Calories from Fat 15 (12%)	Potassium 743mg
Total Fat 2g	Carbohydrates 28g
Saturated Fat 0g	Sugar 7g
Cholesterol 0mg	Protein 3g

ROSY CELERY SOUP WITH CORN

This creamy soup, packed with vegetables, is perfect for a light lunch or the start of a meal.

1 ½ cups (375 mL) chopped celery
1 cup (250 mL) chopped onion
1 clove garlic, minced
2 tsp (10 mL) olive oil
1 plum tomato, finely diced
1 ½ tbsp (22 mL) all-purpose flour
2 ¼ cups (560 mL) water or Golden Vegetable Broth (p. 115)
1 cup (250 mL) 2% evaporated milk
½ cup (125 mL) grated old cheddar cheese
1 ⅓ cups (325 mL) cooked corn kernels
freshly ground black pepper, to taste
pinch of cayenne, optional

Sauté celery, onion and garlic in olive oil in a heavy saucepan over medium heat for about 10 minutes or until they begin to turn golden. Add tomato and continue cooking for a few minutes.

Add flour and cook while stirring for 2 minutes. Stir in water or broth and cook for about 10 minutes or until vegetables are tender. Add milk. Stir in cheese, a bit at a time until it melts. Add corn and seasoning.

Serves 6.

Nutrient Analysis per serving	
Calories 152	Potassium 4 mg
Calories from Fat 57 (37%)	Carbohydrate 3g
Total Fat 6g	Fibre g
Saturated Fat 3g	Sugars
Cholesterol 12mg	Protein
Sodium 141mg	

MUSKOKA FISH CHOWDER

Muskoka Sands, Gravenhurst, ON

Chef Hubert Obermeier has created a delicate chowder with a clear golden broth and an array of fresh vegetables, attractively cut in thin strips or julienned. To julienne vegetables, slice them into matchsticks 1/8 in (3 mm) thick and about 2 in (5 cm) long. The origin of the term is unknown but it has been used for almost 300 years. Chef Hubert chose pickerel, trout and white fish fillets for his chowder; I used haddock and trout.

½ cup (125 mL) julienned carrots
½ cup (125 mL) leek, white part only
¼ cup (60 mL) julienned celery
½ cup (125mL) julienned sweet red pepper
½ cup (125 mL) onion cut in thin slivers
1 tbsp (15 mL) extra-virgin olive oil
6 cups (1.5 L) Golden Vegetable Broth (p. 115)
4 mini red or Yukon gold potatoes, unpeeled and cut 1/8 in (3 mm) thick
1 tbsp (15 mL) chopped fresh thyme
2 tbsp (30 mL) chopped fresh dill
1 tbsp (15 mL) low-sodium soy sauce
½ tsp (2 mL) Worcestershire sauce
1 bay leaf
pinch saffron
freshly ground pepper, to taste
8 oz (250 g) skinless haddock fillet
6 oz (170 g) skinless trout fillet

Sauté carrot, leek, celery, red pepper and onion in large saucepan with olive oil over medium heat, stirring often until softened.

Add broth, potatoes, thyme, dill, soy sauce, Worcestershire sauce, bay leaf, saffron and pepper. Simmer until potatoes are softened.

Cut fish into ½-in (1.2-cm) dice and add to the vegetables. Simmer for a few minutes, just until fish is cooked. Remove bay leaf. Ladle into bowls. Garnish with more chopped dill.

Serves 10, ¾ cup (175 mL) each

Nutrient Analysis per serving	
Calories 134	Potassium 60mg
Calories from Fat 30 (22%)	Carbohydrates 1?g
Total Fat 3g	Fibre 2g
Saturated Fat 1g	Sugar 3g
Cholesterol 23mg	Protein 13g
Sodium 73mg	

CHILLED ZUCCHINI SOUP WITH GARLIC CROUTONS AND DILL

We like to make this refreshing, low-fat soup in the summer when local zucchini are plentiful. You can use any size zucchini, but smaller ones will give a darker green soup. Buttermilk imparts a rich tart flavour in spite of being virtually fat free. Garlic croutons add a little crunch and a burst of flavour.

Chilled Zucchini Soup

2 lb (1 kg) unpeeled zucchini, chopped
1 cup (250 mL) green onions, chopped
2 cloves garlic, crushed
1 tbsp (15 mL) olive oil
1 tbsp (15 mL) curry powder
1 tbsp (15 mL) cumin
2 cups (500 mL) vegetable broth
3 cups (750 mL) buttermilk
1/2 tsp (2 mL) freshly ground pepper
chopped fresh dill for garnish

Garlic Croutons

3 slices bread, crust removed
½ tbsp (7 mL) olive oil
⅛ tsp (½ mL) garlic powder

For the soup:

Sauté zucchini, onions and garlic in olive oil in a heavy pot over medium heat for about 7 minutes or until zucchini is softened, stirring occasionally. Stir in curry and cumin and cook 2 minutes longer. Add broth, bring to a boil and simmer for 10 minutes. Remove from heat and let cool for 20 minutes.

Purée soup in a blender in several batches. Pour into a large bowl and stir in buttermilk and pepper. Chill for at least hours. Serve topped with garlic croutons and fresh dill.

Serves 8.

For the croutons:

Cut bread into small cubes about ½ in (1 cm) and place in a small bowl. Drizzle oil and sprinkle garlic powder over top. Toss lightly to coat. Bake at 375°F (190°C) for about 10 minutes or until browned. Set aside to cool.

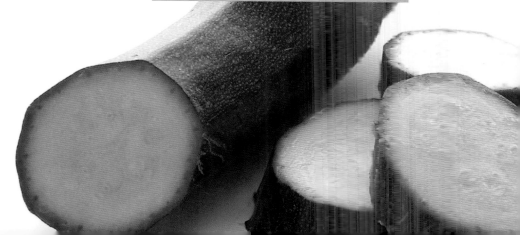

Nutrient Analysis per serving:	
Calories 95	Potassium 55m
Calories from Fat 22 (24%)	Carbohydrates 1g
Total Fat 3g	Fibre 2g
Saturated Fat 0g	Sugar 8g
Cholesterol 2mg	Protein 2g
Sodium 73mg	

DESSERTS

APRICOT MOUSSE WITH GRAND MARNIER

Sunny dried apricots, rich in potassium, make a great dessert when combined with whipped egg whites and orange liqueur.

6 oz (170 g) dried apricots
water to cover, about 1 cup (250 mL)
2 tbsp (30 mL) Grand Marnier
3 large egg whites at room temperature
6 thin orange wedges
6 sprigs of mint

Combine apricots and water in a saucepan and bring to a boil. Reduce heat and simmer, covered until tender, about 15 minutes. Cool apricots in their liquid. Purée apricots, liquid and Grand Marnier in a food processor or blender.

Beat egg whites until stiff but not dry with an electric mixer. Gently fold a couple of spoonfuls of egg whites into the apricot purée, just until white disappears. Fold remaining egg whites into the apricots until evenly blended.

Spoon into 6 wine or martini glasses. Garnish with orange wedges and a sprig of mint.

Serves 6.

Nutrient Analysis per serving:

Calories 124	Potassium 513 mg
Calories from Fat 2 (2%)	Carbohydrates 27 g
Total Fat <1g	Fibre 4 g
Saturated Fat 0g	Sugar 17 g
Cholesterol 0mg	Protein 3 g
Sodium 34mg	

AUNT HELEN'S CRANBERRY AND ORANGE OATMEAL SQUARES

My Aunt Helen Smith from French Lake, NB, baked up a big batch of these tasty squares for a family reunion. I have added orange zest and cranberries to give a nice tartness. Low in fat and sodium, they are sure to satisfy your sweet tooth.

½ cup (125 mL) rolled oats
⅓ cup (75 mL) chopped dates
½ cup (125 mL) boiling water
¼ cup (60 mL) soft margarine
½ cup (125 mL) brown sugar
1 egg, beaten
1 tsp (5 mL) grated orange zest
1 cup (250 mL) flour
½ tsp (2 mL) baking powder
½ tsp (2 mL) soda
½ tsp (2 mL) vanilla
1 cup (250 mL) chopped cranberries
¼ cup (60 mL) flaked coconut
¼ cup (60 mL) chopped nuts
powdered sugar

Combine rolled oats, dates and water in a small bowl. Set aside to cool.

Cream margarine and sugar. Beating, add orange zest and oat mixture. Sift flour, baking powder and soda. Stir into batter; batter will be stiff. Add vanilla, cranberries, coconut and nuts.

Spread evenly in a 9-in (23-cm) square greased pan and bake at 350°F (175°C) for about 25 minutes. Let cool, then dust with powdered sugar.

Cut into 36 pieces, 1 ½-in (4-cm) square.

Nutrient Analysis per serving:	
Calories 56	Potassium 36mg
Calories from Fat 20 (35%)	Carbohydrates 9g
Total Fat 2g	Fibre 1g
Saturated Fat 0g	Sugar 6g
Cholesterol 6mg	Protein 1g
Sodium 38mg	

BAKED APPLES WITH DATES AND NUTS

My husband John is not especially fond of baked apples but he thought this version with dates and nuts was something special. Choose good baking apples such as Gravensteins or Cortlands for this delicious, simple, low-fat dessert. Apples are a rich source of antioxidants, minerals and vitamins as well as soluble fibre that can help lower cholesterol.

6 apples
¼ cup (60 mL) finely chopped dates
¼ cup (60 mL) finely chopped toasted walnuts or pecans
1 tbsp (15 mL) orange juice concentrate, thawed
1 cup (250 mL) apple juice
¼ tsp (1 mL) cinnamon
2 tsp (10 mL) honey
freshly grated nutmeg
vegetable oil spray

Core apples, leaving ½ in (1.2 cm) at the bottom. Peel around the top.

Combine dates, nuts and orange juice concentrate in a small bowl. Stuff apples and spray tops with vegetable oil spray. Arrange in an 8 x 8-in (20 x 20-cm) or 9 x 9-in (23 x 23-cm) baking dish depending on the size of the apples.

Heat apple juice to boiling in a microwave oven. Stir in cinnamon and pour around apples. Bake at 350°F (175°C) for about 45 minutes or until apples are tender, basting several times with juice.

Just before serving, baste again with juice and drizzle honey over apples. Grate a little nutmeg over top for extra flavour. Serve warm or at room temperature.

Serves 6.

Nutrient Analysis per serving:

Calories 157	Potassium 295mg
Calories from Fat 29 (19%)	Carbohydrates 34g
Total Fat 3g	Fibre 4g
Saturated Fat 0g	Sugar 23g
Cholesterol 0mg	Protein 1g
Sodium 3mg	

EASY APPLE STRUDEL

Apple strudel or apfelstrudel is a traditional Viennese dessert. Sweet apples combined with raisins, nuts, brown sugar and cinnamon make a wonderful filling for flaky pastry made from flour, butter and salt. In this version, calories and fat are reduced by using phyllo (filo) dough sheets sprayed lightly with vegetable oil. Frozen phyllo dough is available at most grocery stores.

4 medium apples such as Cortlands or Gravensteins
2 tsp (10 mL) grated lemon zest
¼ cup (60 mL) golden raisins
2 tbsp (30 mL) chopped walnuts or almonds
½ tsp (2 mL) cinnamon
pinch of grated nutmeg
¼ cup (60 mL) brown sugar
6 sheets phyllo dough
vegetable oil spray
1 tsp (5 mL) soft margarine, melted
1 tsp (5 mL) coarse sugar

Peel and core apples, cut into ⅜-in (5 mm) dice. Toss with lemon zest, raisins, nuts, cinnamon, nutmeg and sugar.

Thaw phyllo dough and carefully remove one sheet. Cover remaining dough with a damp towel so it doesn't dry out. Place sheet on a counter with the long side facing you. Spray with vegetable oil. Place a second sheet of phyllo over first and spray with oil. Repeat with a third layer.

Spoon half of the apple mixture in a 4-in (10-cm) strip along the long side of the dough nearest you, 1 in (2.5 cm) from the edge. Roll it up firmly like a jelly roll. Tuck the ends under. Repeat steps to make the second strudel. Place each one, seam side down, diagonally on a separate baking sheet.

Brush tops with melted margarine and sprinkle with sugar. Bake at 375°F (190°C) for about 30 minutes or until golden brown and crisp. Serve hot as pastry will soften upon cooling, slicing on the diagonal.

Makes 2 strudels. Serves 10.

Nutrient Analysis per serving:	
Calories 112	Potassium 118mg
Calories from Fat 23 (21%)	Carbohydrate 22g
Total Fat 3g	Fiber 1g
Saturated Fat 0g	Sugar 13
Cholesterol 0mg	Protein 1g
Sodium 61mg	

OLD-FASHIONED APPLESAUCE

Freshly prepared warm applesauce makes a quick dessert or tangy side dish for pork. Gravenstein and Cortland apples cook up well and have excellent flavour, especially when topped with a shake of cinnamon or nutmeg. If you drop the cut-up apples into cold water they won't discolour. Make up a big batch in the autumn when local apples are at their best and freeze it in small containers to enjoy throughout the year. If using older apples, add a little fresh lemon juice. Sweeten with honey or maple syrup, if desired. If you like a very smooth sauce, you can cook chunks of unpared and uncored apples until tender and put them through a food mill.

6 large apples, about 2 lb (1 kg)
½ to ¾ cups (125 to 175 mL) water

Pare and core apples and cut into chunks. Place in a saucepan and add water.

Bring to a boil over high heat. Cover and reduce heat to medium low. Simmer for 5 to 20 minutes, stirring occasionally, until apples are very tender, breaking up chunks with a wooden spoon. Add more water if sauce is too thick.

Serves 6, ½ cup (125 mL) each

Nutrient Analysis per serving:

Calories 73	Potassium 136mg
Calories from Fat 0	Carbohydrates 19g
Total Fat 0g	Fibre 2g
Saturated Fat 0g	Sugar 15g
Cholesterol 0mg	Protein <1g
Sodium 1mg	

GINGERED FRUIT COMPOTE

Elaine Elliot and Virginia Lee

Tart, fresh lime tempers the sweetness of this variation on fruit salad. It can serve double duty at breakfast and dessert time and is flexible when it comes to ingredients.

2 cups (500 mL) blueberries
2 cups (500 mL) fresh pineapple, cubed
1 large orange, segmented and with the white pith removed
1 tbsp (15 mL) diced crystallized ginger
1 ½ tbsp (22 mL) liquid honey
1 tbsp (15 mL) lime juice
zest of 1 lime

Combine fruit and ginger in a serving bowl. Blend honey, lime juice and lime zest in a small bowl; pour over fruit and stir to combine. Serve chilled or at room temperature.

Serves 5, 1 cup (250 mL) each.

Nutrient Analysis per serving:

Calories 103	Potassium 172mg
Calories from Fat 3 (3%)	Carbohydrates 27g
Total Fat <1g	Fibre 3g
Saturated Fat 0g	Protein 1g
Cholesterol 0mg	
Sodium 2mg	

CREAMY RICE PUDDING WITH CINNAMON

Rice pudding is a classic dessert in many European countries; we always order it in Greek restaurants and luxuriate in its smooth, creamy texture. My challenge was to make a rich-tasting low-fat version; but how can rice pudding made with skimmed milk be creamy? The secret lies in evaporated milk and Arborio rice, which is high in starch. Flavoured with fresh lemon, cinnamon and maple syrup, this dessert will be a big hit.

½ cup (125 mL) uncooked short grain rice
1 cup (250 mL) water
2 strips lemon peel, each ½ x 2 ½ in (13 mm x 6 cm)
3-in (7.5-cm) cinnamon stick
¾ cup (175 mL) 2% evaporated milk
2 ¾ cups (675 mL) skimmed milk
2 tbsp (30 mL) brown sugar
1 tsp (5 mL) cornstarch
2 tbsp (30 mL) maple syrup
⅓ cup (75 mL) golden raisins
1 tsp (5 mL) vanilla, optional
ground cinnamon

Bring rice and water to a boil in a heavy saucepan. Cover and simmer on low heat for 10 minutes. Add lemon peel, cinnamon stick, evaporated milk and 1 ¾ cups (435 mL) of the skimmed milk.

Combine sugar and cornstarch and add remaining cup of milk and maple syrup. Stir into rice mixture. Bring to a boil over medium-low heat and simmer over low heat for 25 minutes. Add raisins and continue cooking for 25 minutes longer until slightly thickened, stirring often.

Remove from heat and discard lemon peel and cinnamon stick. Add vanilla, if using. Serve warm or chilled, sprinkled liberally with cinnamon. Pudding will thicken when chilled.

Serves 8, ½ cup (125 mL) each.

Nutrient Analysis per serving:

Calories 148	Potassium 216mg
Calories from Fat 6 (4%)	Carbohydrates 30g
Total Fat 1g	Fibre 1g
Saturated Fat <1g	Sugar 16g
Cholesterol 2mg	Protein 5g
Sodium 62mg	

EASY BLUEBERRY CRÈME BRÛLÉE

Quaco Inn, St Martins, NB

This new version of crème brûlée is a great dessert! It is easy to make, attractive and flavourful, with the tang of fresh blueberries and yogurt contrasting with the crunch of caramelized sugar on top.

2 cups (500 mL) blueberries
⅔ cup (150 mL) low-fat sour cream, 5% milk fat
½ cup (125 mL) plain fat-free yogurt
⅓ cup (75 mL) brown sugar
mint leaves, as garnish

Divide blueberries among 6 heat-proof ramekins.

Combine sour cream and yogurt and spread evenly over blueberries, being careful to cover completely.

Spread brown sugar over sour cream and broil 3 in (7.5 cm) from element until sugar caramelizes approximately 3 to 5 minutes. Watch carefully, as topping can easily burn. (I used a butane crème brûlée torch to caramelize the sugar. It gives precise control and does the job in seconds.)

Serve immediately, taking care in handling the hot ramekins.

Serves 6.

Nutrient Analysis per serving:

Calories 113	Potassium 106mg
Calories from Fat 21 (18%)	Carbohydrate 22g
Total Fat 2g	Fibre 1g
Saturated Fat 1g	Sugar 17g
Cholesterol 6mg	Protein 2g
Sodium 37mg	

CRISP APPLES WITH CHEDDAR CHEESE AND HONEY

"Surely the apple is the noblest of fruits," wrote Henry David Thoreau in Wild Apples. *A fresh, crisp apple with shiny skin is a delightful gastronomic experience and the basis of this simple dessert. Arrange slices of crisp apples, cheddar cheese, nuts and honey on individual plates. It only takes a few minutes to prepare but is satisfying and delicious.*

1 large crisp apple or 2 small apples
1 oz (30 g) aged low-fat cheddar cheese
2 tbsp (30 mL) coarsely chopped pecans or walnuts
2 tsp (10 mL) honey
cinnamon

Cut apple into quarters; remove core but leave peel on. Slice into thin wedges and arrange in fan-shape on individual plates. Cut cheese into 4 slices and divide between plates.

Scatter nuts over top. Drizzle honey over apples and cheese. Dust with cinnamon.

Serves 2.

Nutrient Analysis per serving:	
Calories 127	Calcium 102mg
Calories from Fat 33 (26%)	Carbohydrates 21g
Total Fat 4g	Fibre 3g
Saturated Fat 1g	Sugar 17g
Cholesterol 3mg	Protein 4g
Sodium 88mg	

RUM-GLAZED PINEAPPLE WITH BLUEBERRIES

How can such a tasty and attractive dessert be so simple to prepare? You can make this intensely flavoured fruit dessert in just a few minutes and it presents beautifully. In addition to blueberries, you could fill the centre with yogurt or a fruit sorbet.

4 slices fresh pineapple ¾ in (2 cm) thick
2 tbsp (30 mL) dark brown sugar
⅓ cup (75 mL) orange juice
3 tbsp (45 mL) dark rum
½ cup (125 mL) fresh blueberries
4 sprigs tarragon or mint

Remove skin from pineapple slices. Cut each slice in half and remove core.

Sprinkle sugar in a non-stick skillet over medium heat. Add pineapple slices and sauté for 5 minutes, turning several times to coat with melted sugar.

Pour orange juice and rum over pineapple and continue cooking for 4 minutes or until sauce begins to thicken.

Carefully transfer 2 half slices to each of 4 individual plates and arrange to form a circle. Fill centre with blueberries and drizzle sauce over top. Garnish with a sprig of tarragon.

Serves 4.

Nutrient Analysis per serving:	
Calories 111	Potassium 182mg
Calories from Fat 2 (2%)	Carbohydrates 22g
Total Fat <1g	Fibre 2g
Saturated Fat 0g	Sugar 18g
Cholesterol 0mg	Protein 1g
Sodium 4mg	

PEPPERED STRAWBERRIES WITH BALSAMIC VINEGAR AND MINT

This is a great summer dessert when strawberries are in season. The unlikely combination of black pepper and balsamic vinegar complements the fruity sweetness of fresh strawberries.

3 cups (750 mL) fresh strawberries, halved
bunch of fresh mint
2 tbsp (30 mL) brown sugar
2 tsp (10 mL) balsamic vinegar
freshly ground black pepper

Place cut strawberries in a bowl. Finely shred 4 mint leaves. Combine brown sugar and balsamic vinegar in a small bowl and stir in shredded mint. Pour over berries and gently toss to cover. Sprinkle with pepper.

Serve in martini or wine glasses topped with a sprig of mint.

Serves 4.

Nutrient Analysis per serving:	
Calories 64	Potassium 209mg
Calories from Fat 3 (5%)	Carbohydrates 16g
Total Fat <1g	Fibre 2g
Saturated Fat 0g	Sugar 12g
Cholesterol 0mg	Protein 1g
Sodium 4mg	

SIDES &
ACCOMPANIMENTS

OVEN-CRISPED HERB TOMATOES

Elaine Elliot and Virginia Lee

This colourful side dish sparks up a plate, whether made with luscious ripe tomatoes in season, or their paler cousins available at other times of year. Elliot and Lee use Herbes de Province, a blend containing rosemary, marjoram, thyme, sage, anise seed and other herbs. Tasty herbs such as oregano and basil also work well.

3 large tomatoes
¾ cup (175 mL) fresh breadcrumbs
2 tsp (10 mL) Herbes de Province
freshly ground pepper
1 tbsp (15 mL) olive oil

Cut tomatoes in half horizontally and arrange them in a shallow baking pan.

Evenly combine breadcrumbs, herbs, pepper and oil in a small bowl. Sprinkle 1 tbsp (15 mL) crumbs on top of each tomato half.

Bake in a preheated 375°F (190°C) oven for 15 to 20 minutes until tomatoes are softened and crumbs are crisped.

Serve on a lettuce-lined plate.

Serves 6.

Nutrient Analysis per serving:

Calories 52	Potassium 234mg
Calories from Fat 23 (44%)	Carbohydrates 7g
Total Fat 3g	Fibre 1g
Saturated Fat 0g	Sugar 3g
Cholesterol 0mg	Protein 1g
Sodium 43mg	

KIERAN'S AND CAM'S SMASHED POTATOES

My grandsons thought these potatoes were terrific. The method of making them is a novel and easy way to make potatoes something out of the ordinary. For most attractive results choose red potatoes.

6 medium red potatoes
vegetable oil spray
freshly ground pepper
herbs of choice
6 tbsp (90 mL) shredded low-fat cheddar cheese

Cook potatoes in boiling water just until tender; drain and set aside. Alternately you can zap them in the microwave for a few minutes until done.

Using a holder or kitchen towel, transfer cooked potatoes to an oiled baking sheet. Take a heavy glass or small bowl and press down firmly on each potato, "smashing" it into a round patty about ¾ in (2 cm) thick.

Spray potatoes lightly with oil and season with pepper and herbs of choice. Sprinkle 1 tbsp (15 mL) cheese on top of each potato and bake for 20 minutes at 425°F (220°C).

Serves 6.

Nutrient Analysis per serving

Calories 118	Potassium 672mg
Calories from Fat 12 (10%)	Carbohydrates 22g
Total Fat 1g	Fibre 5g
Saturated Fat <1g	Sugar 0g
Cholesterol 2mg	Protein 5g
Sodium 58mg	

GOLDEN SUMMER SQUASH WITH THYME AND PARMESAN

This recipe is a way of using a harvest of yellow summer squash. Combined with onions, garlic and Parmesan cheese, the squash cooks down and becomes caramelized during baking.

1 large onion, thinly sliced
1 tbsp (15 mL) olive oil
2 cloves garlic, minced
3 or 4 small golden summer squash, about 1 ½ lb (750 g), thinly sliced
2 tsp (10 mL) fresh thyme or ¾ tsp (4 mL) dry thyme
pepper to taste
2 tbsp (30 mL) grated Parmesan cheese

Sauté onion in oil in an oven-proof skillet until golden, about 10 minutes. Add garlic, summer squash, thyme and pepper.

Stir-fry until the squash slices soften and start to brown. Cover with aluminum foil and bake at 375°F (190°C) for 20 minutes. Remove and discard foil. Sprinkle Parmesan cheese over top and bake for 20 minutes or until liquid is absorbed and cheese browns.

Serves 4.

Nutrient Analysis per serving:

Calories 78	Potassium 503mg
Calories from Fat 36 (46%)	Carbohydrates 10g
Total Fat 4g	Fibre 2g
Saturated Fat 1g	Sugar 5g
Cholesterol 1mg	Protein 3g
Sodium 38mg	

HONEYED CARROTS WITH GRAND MARNIER AND FRESH CILANTRO

Amherst Shore Country Inn, Lorneville, NS

These tasty carrots approach gourmet status with the easy addition of Grand Marnier and orange zest.

2 cups (500 mL) fresh carrots, in sticks or sliced diagonally
2 tsp (10 mL) olive oil
1 tsp (5 mL) honey
1 tbsp (15 mL) Grand Marnier liqueur
1 tsp (5 mL) finely grated orange zest
2 tbsp (30 mL) fresh cilantro, chopped, as garnish

Pare and cut carrots into preferred shape and cook until tender. Drain and set aside.

Combine oil, honey, liqueur and orange zest in a small skillet or saucepan. Add carrots and stir to coat evenly. Keep warm over low heat.

Serve sprinkled with chopped cilantro.

Serves 4.

Nutrient Analysis per serving:

Calories 65	Potassium 209mg
Calories from Fat 20 (31%)	Carbohydrates 9g
Total Fat 2g	Fibre 2g
Saturated Fat 0g	Sugar 4g
Cholesterol 0mg	Protein 1g
Sodium 44mg	

TZATZIKI WITH MINT AND GARLIC

This classic Greek condiment is made with thick yogurt, shredded cucumber, garlic and fresh mint. Some versions also add lemon, parsley and fresh dill instead of mint. It can be served as a sauce with meat or fish, or as a dip with pita bread and raw vegetables. The secret to making thick tzatziki lies in draining excess moisture from yogurt and grated cucumbers. Usually tzatziki is seasoned with salt but this version is refreshing without it.

2 cups (500 mL) fat-free plain yogurt
1 medium cucumber
2 cloves garlic, minced
1 tbsp (15 mL) or more fresh mint, finely chopped
freshly ground pepper

To thicken the yogurt, spoon it into a large coffee filter nested in a sieve over a bowl. Refrigerate for several hours or overnight to allow excess liquid to drain off, leaving thick, creamy yogurt "cheese." Discard liquid and transfer thickened yogurt to a bowl.

Peel cucumber and coarsely grate it, discarding seeds. Gently squeeze out moisture with your hands over the sink. Then blot cucumber with paper towels until most of its juice has been removed. Stir cucumber into yogurt.

Add garlic, mint and pepper. Cover and refrigerate until ready to serve.

Serves 8, about 1 cup (250 mL) each.

Nutrient Analysis per serving:	
Calories 61	Potassium 270mg
Calories from Fat 12 (20%)	Carbohydrates 8g
Total Fat 1g	Fibre <1g
Saturated Fat 1g	Sugar 1g
Cholesterol 5mg	Protein 5g
Sodium 59mg	

FRAGRANT COCONUT RICE AND BEANS WITH SWEET POTATO

Many cultures have traditional recipes for cooking rice and beans, but this version is unusual in that it is made with low-fat coconut milk and uses black beans and edamame soy beans. For convenience, I buy frozen soy beans in the pod and shell them. This recipe is an adaptation of one published by Jim Romanoff of Associated Press.

2 tsp (10 mL) olive oil
1 cup (250 mL) peeled sweet potato cut in 1/4-in (6-mm) dice
2 tsp (10 mL) finely minced fresh ginger
½ cup (125 mL) chopped green onions
1 ¼ cups (310 mL) jasmine rice
1 15-oz (425 mL) can low-fat coconut milk
1 cup (250 mL) water
1 tbsp (15 mL) low-sodium soy sauce
1 ½ tbsp (22 mL) fresh lime juice
1 ¼ cups (310 mL) cooked black beans
½ cup (125 mL) shelled cooked edamame
1 tsp (5 mL) grated lime zest
¼ cup (60 mL) unsalted peanuts, chopped

Heat olive oil in a large, heavy saucepan and cook sweet potato, ginger and green onions over medium heat for about 5 minutes, stirring occasionally.

Add rice and stir-fry for a minute. Stir in coconut milk, water, soy sauce and lime juice and bring to a boil. Reduce heat to simmer, cover and cook for about 20 minutes until liquid is absorbed and rice is tender.

Fluff rice with a fork and gently mix in black beans, edamame and lime zest. Heat for a few minutes. Sprinkle peanuts over top.

Serves 8, about 1 cup (250 mL) each.

Nutrient Analysis per serving:

Calories 237	Potassium 405mg
Calories from Fat 58 (25%)	Carbohydrates 37g
Total Fat 7g	Fibre 4g
Saturated Fat 3g	Sugar 2g
Cholesterol 0mg	Protein 8g
Sodium 88mg	

FOUR-GRAIN PILAF WITH CURRANTS AND CRANBERRIES

This combination of barley, millet, wild rice and brown rice with currants and cranberries makes a versatile side dish. Leftovers freeze well and can be heated in the microwave.

¾ cup (175 mL) currants
½ cup (125 mL) dried cranberries
¼ cup (60 mL) orange juice
2 tsp (10 mL) olive oil
½ cup (125 mL) finely chopped red onion
1 tsp (5 mL) minced garlic
½ cup (125 mL) pearl barley
¼ cup (60 mL) millet
½ cup (125 mL) wild rice
½ cup (125 mL) brown basmati rice
3 cups (750 mL) Golden Vegetable Broth (p. 115) or
   low-sodium chicken broth
½ cup (125 mL) chopped green onions or chives
1 cup (250 mL) chopped parsley
freshly ground pepper to taste

Soak currants and cranberries in orange juice. Heat a large heavy saucepan or Dutch oven and add olive oil and onions. Sauté for 5 minutes; then add garlic, barley, millet, wild rice and brown rice. Stir and cook for a few minutes to coat grains with oil.

Pour in broth and bring to a boil. Reduce heat and simmer covered for 30 minutes or until tender. Fluff with a fork and stir in soaked currants and cranberries. Add green onions and parsley and season with pepper.

Serves 14, ½ cup (125 mL) each.

Nutrient Analysis per serving:

Calories 135	Potassium 259mg
Calories from Fat 13 (10%)	Carbohydrates 28g
Total Fat 2g	Fibre 3g
Saturated Fat 0g	Sugar 7g
Cholesterol 0mg	Protein 3g
Sodium 15mg	

STEAMED WHITE RICE

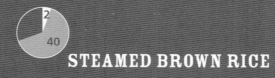

STEAMED BROWN RICE

When first married, I tried unsuccessfully to cook rice that was light and fluffy. It always came out sticky and mushy. Using converted rice partly solved the problem, but the grains were not very tender. In frustration, I asked a Chinese friend to tell me the secret of making perfect rice and her reply was simple: wash the rice to remove the surface starch, don't use too much water in cooking and no salt. Her recommendation worked like a charm. Use a heavy bottomed saucepan with tight-fitting lid for best results.

1 cup (250 mL) long-grain rice
1 ½ cups (375 mL) cold water

Put the rice in a saucepan and run cold water over it, swirling gently with your hand. Pour off the water and repeat several times until the rinse water is clear. Drain well. Add 1 ½ cups (375 mL) water to drained rice and bring to a boil uncovered over high heat. Reduce heat to very low; cover the pot and let steam for 15 to 20 minutes. Do not uncover during cooking. Fluff with a fork before serving.

Serves 6, ½ cup (125 mL) each.

Nutrient Analysis per serving:	
Calories 113	Potassium 35mg
Calories from Fat 2 (2%)	Carbohydrates 25g
Total Fat 0g	Fibre <1g
Saturated Fat 0g	Sugar 0g
Cholesterol 0mg	Protein 2g
Sodium 3mg	

Brown rice has bran surrounding the kernel which makes it nuttier, chewier and higher in nutrients than white rice. It has a shorter shelf life, so it is a good idea to keep it refrigerated. For softer rice, add an extra ½ cup (125 mL) water. Leftover rice freezes well and can be reheated in a microwave.

1 cup (250 mL) brown long-grain basmati rice
2 cups (500 mL) water

Rinse and drain rice. Place rice and water in a saucepan. Bring to a boil, cover tightly and cook over low heat for about 40 minutes or until rice is tender and liquid has been absorbed. Do not stir during cooking. Fluff with a fork.

Serves 6, ½ cup (125 mL) each.

Nutrient Analysis per serving:	
Calories 114	Potassium 69mg
Calories from Fat 8 (7%)	Carbohydrates 24g
Total Fat 1g	Fibre 1g
Saturated Fat 0g	Sugar 0g
Cholesterol 0mg	Protein 2g
Sodium 4mg	

TANGY RAINBOW SLAW

COOL CUCUMBER AND RED ONION SALAD WITH HONEY AND DILL

This colourful, piquant, fat-free cabbage salad is a great partner with Blackened Fish Soft Tacos (p. 78) and will liven up any meal.

1 ½ cups (375 mL) finely shredded green cabbage
1 ½ cups (375 mL) finely shredded purple cabbage
1 medium shredded carrot
¼ cup (60 mL) finely diced red pepper
1 or 2 green peppers, chopped
¼ cup (60 mL) chopped cilantro
2 tbsp (30 mL) or more fresh lime juice

Combine vegetables in a bowl and toss with lime juice.

Serves 6.

Nutrient Analysis per serving:	
Calories 24	Potassium 205mg
Calories from Fat 1 (5%)	Carbohydrates 6g
Total Fat 0g	Fibre 2g
Saturated Fat 0g	Sugar 3g
Cholesterol 0mg	Protein 1g
Sodium 19mg	

This fresh, crisp salad can be assembled in minutes and goes well with salmon dishes. The beauty of using an English cucumber is that it doesn't have to be peeled and the green skin contrasts nicely with red onion. This salad will keep in the fridge several days.

½ English cucumber, thinly sliced
½ red onion or sweet Vidalia onion, thinly sliced
⅓ cup (75 mL) cider vinegar or rice vinegar
2 tbsp (30 mL) cold water
1 tbsp (15 mL) honey
freshly ground black pepper
2 tbsp (30 mL) coarsely chopped fresh dill

Place cucumber and onion slices in a serving dish. Combine vinegar, water, honey and pepper in a small bowl. Pour over vegetables and stir to coat evenly. Top with fresh dill.

Serves 4.

Nutrient Analysis per serving:	
Calories 35	Potassium 136mg
Calories from Fat 1 (2%)	Carbohydrates 5g
Total Fat 0g	Fibre 1g
Saturated Fat 0g	Sugar 6g
Cholesterol 0mg	Protein 1g
Sodium 3mg	

RADICCHIO AND ENDIVE SALAD WITH MAPLE PEACH DRESSING

The Briars Resort, Jackson's Point, ON

Chef Trevor Ledlie has created a memorable salad with this combination of fruit and interesting greens. His maple and peach dressing is particularly imaginative. I reduced the amount of oil in the dressing and added blueberries, extra pears and walnuts to the salad.

Radicchio and endive salad

2 Belgian endives, separated into leaves
2 butterhead lettuces or 1 small Romaine lettuce
1 radicchio
2 thinly sliced pears
½ cup (125 mL) blueberries
¼ cup (60 mL) toasted walnuts, coarsely chopped
6 sprigs of mint

Maple peach dressing

I have substituted apple and orange juice for some of the oil and vinegar in the original recipe.

4 tbsp (60 mL) apple juice
2 tbsp (30 mL) white wine vinegar
2 tbsp (30 mL) orange juice
4 tbsp (60 mL) maple syrup
2 large peaches, peeled and pitted
½ tsp (2 mL) jalapeño pepper, chopped
1 tsp (5 mL) chopped parsley
fresh lime juice, to taste
2 tbsp (30 mL) olive or grape seed oil

For the salad

Arrange endive leaves and butterhead lettuce around the outside of six plates. Slice radicchio and place in the centre.

Drizzle with Maple Peach Dressing and arrange pears and blueberries on top. Scatter nuts over fruit and garnish with mint.

For the dressing

Combine all ingredients in a blender and process until pureed.

Serves 6.

Nutrient Analysis per serving:	
Calories 139	Potassium 306mg
Calories from Fat 52 (38%)	Carbohydrates 22g
Total Fat 6g	Fibre 3g
Saturated Fat 1g	Sugar 15g
Cholesterol 0mg	Protein 2g
Sodium 4mg	

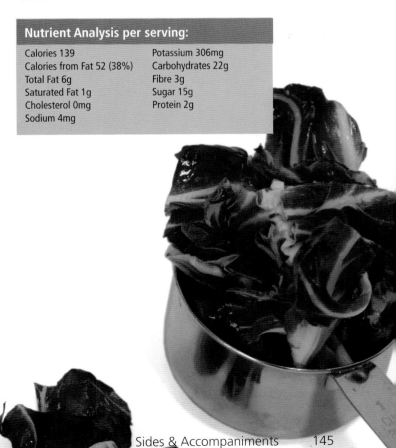

TOMATO SALSA

Dalvay-by-the-Sea, PEI

This refreshing salsa was created by the chef at Dalvay-by-the-Sea to accompany Cajun Spiced Salmon with Roasted Seaweed (p.90). It would also enhance grilled chicken and other fish dishes.

4 firm tomatoes, peeled, seeded and finely chopped
1 small Spanish or red onion, finely chopped
1 tsp (5 mL) each, coriander, basil, chives, chopped
1 tsp (5 mL) garlic, crushed
1 tsp (5 mL) Dijon mustard
1 tbsp (15 mL) wine vinegar
1 tbsp (15 mL) balsamic vinegar
1 tsp (5 mL) olive oil
freshly ground pepper, to taste

Combine tomatoes and onion in a bowl and mix well. Whisk together remaining ingredients until they are emulsified. Pour over tomatoes and stir well. Cover and refrigerate to let flavours combine.

Serves 4, generously. Makes 2 cups (500 mL).

Nutrient Analysis per serving:	
Calories 51	Potassium 292mg
Calories from Fat 17 (33%)	Carbohydrates 8g
Total Fat 2g	Fibre 2g
Saturated Fat 0g	Sugar 4g
Cholesterol 0mg	Protein 1g
Sodium 22mg	

PEACH AND PEPPER SALSA

Bluenose Lodge, Lunenburg, NS

This salsa was created at the Bluenose Lodge to go with their pan-fried Haddock Fillets (p. 20). It is colourful and will stimulate your taste buds. If you love peaches, add an extra one to the mix.

½ cup (125 mL) fresh peaches, finely diced
¼ cup (60 mL) onion, finely diced
½ cup (125 mL) red pepper, finely diced
1 tsp (5 mL) jalapeño pepper, finely diced (or 2 shakes Tabasco sauce)
1 tbsp (15 mL) fresh cilantro or parsley, chopped
1 tbsp (15 mL) fresh lime juice

Combine all ingredients and refrigerate 1 to 2 hours to blend flavours.

Makes 1 ¼ cups (310 mL), serves 4.

Nutrient Analysis per serving:	
Calories 19	Potassium 106mg
Calories from Fat 0	Carbohydrates 5g
Total Fat 0g	Fibre 1g
Saturated Fat 0g	Sugar 3g
Cholesterol 0mg	Protein 1g
Sodium 1mg	

RED AND GREEN SALAD WITH RASPBERRY VINAIGRETTE

Cooper's Inn and Restaurant, Shelburne, NS

This lovely, easy-to-prepare salad comes from Cooper's Inn, a registered heritage property from 1784 in historic Loyalist Shelburne, Nova Scotia. Owner-chef Allan Redmond has created it with a variety of colourful greens dressed with oil-free raspberry vinaigrette. He uses several types of lettuce such as green and red leaf, romaine, radicchio and Boston lettuce and garnishes dishes with flowers from his garden.

Salad
mixed red and green lettuce to serve 6

Raspberry Vinaigrette
¼ cup (60 mL) raspberry vinegar
1 tbsp (15 mL) honey
1 or 2 cloves garlic, minced
1 tsp (5 mL) Worcestershire sauce
1 tsp (5 mL) Dijon mustard
1 tsp (5 mL) lemon juice
freshly ground pepper, to taste
½ cup (125 mL) water
2 tbsp (30 mL) freshly grated Parmesan cheese
freshly ground pepper
¼ cup (60 mL) golden raisins
1 tbsp (15 mL) dried currants
6 lemon slices
18 fresh raspberries

For the salad
Prepare salad greens and reserve.

For the vinaigrette
Combine vinegar, honey, garlic, Worcestershire sauce, mustard, lemon juice and pepper in a blender or glass jar.

Add water and process or shake until vinaigrette is well blended.

Toss greens with a little of the vinaigrette and arrange on individual plates that have been sprinkled with Parmesan cheese and freshly ground pepper.

Scatter raisins and currants over top. Garnish with a lemon slice and raspberries. Serve extra dressing on the side.

Serves 6.

Nutrient Analysis per serving:	
Calories 68	Potassium 233mg
Calories from Fat 11 (16%)	Carbohydrates 13g
Total Fat <1g	Fibre 2g
Saturated Fat 1g	Sugar 8g
Cholesterol 3mg	Protein 3g
Sodium 30mg	

RHUBARB CHUTNEY

SPINACH AND MUSHROOMS WITH SEASONED OIL

This chutney combines great texture and taste and brings raves at our table. Serve as a relish with ham, pork, duck or chicken. You can store it in the refrigerator for up to one month.

6 tbsp (90 mL) packed brown sugar
⅓ cup (75 mL) cider vinegar
¼ cup (60 mL) water
¼ tsp (1 mL) dry mustard
½ tsp (2 mL) ground cinnamon
⅛ tsp (0.5 mL) ground cloves
½ cup (125 mL) chopped onions
⅓ cup (75 mL) raisins
2 cups (500 mL) rhubarb cut in ½-in (1.2-cm) slices
⅔ cup (150 mL) chopped dates

Combine brown sugar, vinegar, water, mustard, cinnamon and cloves in a saucepan with a heavy bottom. Bring to a boil over medium heat, stirring until sugar dissolves. Gently boil uncovered for 5 minutes.

Stir in onions and raisins; return to a boil, reduce heat and simmer, covered, for 20 minutes. Add rhubarb and dates; return to a boil and gently simmer uncovered for 10 minutes or until thick, stirring occasionally. Some pieces of rhubarb should still be intact.

Makes 2 ¼ cups (560 mL). A serving is 2 tbsp (30 mL).

Nutrient Analysis per serving:

Calories 51	Potassium 133mg
Calories from Fat <1 (1%)	Carbohydrates 13g
Total Fat 0g	Fibre 1g
Saturated Fat 0g	Sugar 11g
Cholesterol 0mg	Protein <1g
Sodium 4mg	

This easy stir-fry can be made in a few minutes. Vary the dish with different flavoured oils, such as walnut oil, truffle oil, sesame oil or hot chili oil.

1 tbsp (15 mL) olive oil
6 oz (170 g) sliced crimini or button mushrooms
1 clove garlic, minced, optional
¼ cup (60 mL) chopped shallots or red or green onions
9 oz (255 g) fresh baby spinach
freshly ground pepper
1 tsp (5 mL) flavoured oil

Heat oil in a large skillet over medium-high heat. Add mushrooms and sauté for a few minutes until liquid cooks off. Add garlic and onion and stir-fry until mushrooms are browned. Gradually add spinach, stirring until it wilts before adding more.

Sauté until spinach is tender. Season with pepper and flavoured oil.

Serves 4.

Nutrient Analysis per serving:

Calories 72	Potassium 583mg
Calories from Fat 42 (59%)	Carbohydrates 6g
Total Fat 5g	Fibre 2g
Saturated Fat 1g	Sugar 1g
Cholesterol 0mg	Protein 3g
Sodium 54mg	

YOGURT AND CAPER DRESSING

This dressing goes well with Cornmeal-Crusted Salmon Cakes served on a bun (p. 74).

¼ cup (60 mL) fat-free plain yogurt
¼ cup (60 mL) low-fat mayonnaise
1 tsp (5 mL) chopped capers

Whisk ingredients together and serve over salmon cakes.

Makes ½ cup (125 mL). A serving is 1 tbsp (15 mL).

Nutrient Analysis per serving:

Calories 27	Potassium 18mg
Calories from Fat 22 (80%)	Carbohydrates 1g
Total Fat 3g	Fibre 0g
Saturated Fat 0g	Sugar 0g
Cholesterol 3mg	Protein <1g
Sodium 79mg	

LINDA'S WATERMELON SALAD WITH FRESH BASIL AND FETA CHEESE

This recipe from Linda Macintosh is an unusual and refreshing salad. It is easy to prepare and makes a fine addition to any meal. You can vary it by using fresh lime juice instead of vinegar, and mint to replace basil. For a special occasion, cut watermelon into balls instead of cubes and serve the salad in martini glasses. Linda says to prepare the salad shortly before serving so that the watermelon stays crisp. Garnish with roasted pumpkin seeds if you like.

4 cups (1 L) watermelon cubes
1 tbsp (15 mL) balsamic vinegar
1 tbsp (15 mL) chopped fresh basil
1 tbsp (15 mL) crumbled feta cheese

Cut watermelon into 1-in (2.5-cm) cubes and place in a bowl. Sprinkle with balsamic vinegar and fresh basil; toss to coat. Transfer to serving dish and sprinkle cheese over top.

Serves 4.

Nutrient Analysis per serving:

Calories 53	Potassium 181mg
Calories from Fat 6 (12%)	Carbohydrates 12g
Total Fat 1g	Fibre 1g
Saturated Fat 0g	Sugar 10g
Cholesterol 2mg	Protein 1g
Sodium 28mg	

SPICY EAST INDIAN CABBAGE

Stir-frying brings out the sweetness of cabbage which makes it appealing to people who usually do not like it. The addition of onion, peppers, mustard seeds and coconut creates a dish that goes well with roast chicken and curries.

1 tbsp (15 mL) oil
½ tsp (2 mL) mustard seeds
⅛ tsp (½ mL) crushed chili peppers or cayenne
4 tbsp (60 mL) green or red pepper, finely diced
1 large onion, chopped
½ cup (125 mL) unsweetened flaked coconut
½ medium cabbage thinly sliced, about 8 cups (2 L)
½ tsp (2 mL) balsamic vinegar
1 tsp (5 mL) fresh lime juice
 freshly ground black pepper, to taste
3 tbsp (45 mL) chopped green onions

Heat oil in a large wok or heavy frying pan. Add mustard seeds and cover for a minute or two, shaking the pan a few times until the seeds burst. Add peppers and onions and stir over medium heat until onions are golden. Mix in coconut and stir for 2 minutes. Add cabbage and stir-fry for about 5 minutes.

Reduce heat to low, cover and cook 12 to 15 minutes until cabbage is crispy tender, stirring occasionally. Adjust seasoning with vinegar, lime juice and pepper. Toss well. Serve garnished with green onions

Serves 10, ½ cup (125 mL) each.

Nutrient Analysis per serving:

Calories 44	Potassium 182mg
Calories from Fat 21 (48%)	Carbohydrates 5g
Total Fat 2g	Fibre 2g
Saturated Fat 1g	Sugar 3g
Cholesterol 0mg	Protein 1g
Sodium 11mg	

DASH FUNDAMENTALS

WHAT TO EAT ON THE DASH DIET

How does the DASH diet compare with Canada's Food Guide?

The DASH diet is very similar to the diet recommended in Canada's Food Guide to Healthy Eating, published by Health Canada and endorsed by the Heart and Stroke Foundation of Canada. The table compares the number of servings per day of different food categories recommended by DASH and the Canada Food Guide. The main difference is that DASH has lower levels of fat and salt.

Food Group	DASH	Canada's Food Guide
Grains and grain products	6 to 8	6 to 8
Vegetables	4 to 5	7 to 10
Fruits	4 to 5	included with vegetables
Low-fat dairy products	2 to 3	2 to 3
Meat and alternatives	6 or less (1 oz, 30 g)	2 to 3 (2.5 oz, 75 g servings)
Fats	2 to 3 (1 tsp, 5 mL)	2 to 3 (1 tbsp, 15 mL servings)
Nuts, seeds and legumes	4 to 5 per week	Included with meats
Sweets	5 per week	Not specified

These values are based on a 2000 to 2100 calorie-a-day diet for an adult.

DAILY NUTRIENT GOALS

(USED IN THE DASH STUDIES FOR A 2100 CALORIE EATING PLAN)

Total fat	27% of calories
Saturated fat	6% of calories
Protein	18% of calories
Carbohydrates	55% of calories
Cholesterol	150 mg
Sodium	1500 to 2300 mg*
Potassium	4700 mg
Calcium	1250 mg
Fibre	30 g

*Researchers recommend that most people should consume less than 2300 mg of sodium a day. Middle-aged and older individuals who already have high blood pressure should limit sodium to no more than 1500 mg.

WHAT IS ONE DASH SERVING?

FOOD GROUP	SERVING SIZE
Grains and grain products	1 slice of bread, preferably whole grain ½ pita bread or ½ tortilla ½ medium-sized bagel ½ cup (125 mL) cooked cereal, pasta or rice 1 oz (30 g) cold cereal, such as bran flakes 2 graham crackers or 4 soda crackers
Vegetables	1 cup (250 mL) raw leafy vegetables ½ cup (125 mL) cooked vegetables ½ cup (125 mL) vegetable juice
Fruits	1 medium fruit ½ cup (125 mL) fresh, frozen or canned fruit ¾ cup (175 mL) fruit juice ¼ cup (60 mL) dried fruit
Low-fat dairy products	1 cup (250 mL) milk 1 cup (250 mL) yogurt 1 ½ oz (45 g) cheese
Meat, poultry and fish	1 oz (30 g) portion
Nuts, seeds and legumes	⅓ cup (75 mL) or 1 ½ oz (45 g) nuts 2 tbsp (30 mL) or 1 ½ oz (45 g) seeds ½ cup (125 ml) cooked dried beans/legumes 2 tbsp (30 mL) peanut butter 3 oz (85 g) tofu
Fats and oils	1 tsp (5 mL) soft margarine or vegetable oil 1 tsp (5 mL) regular mayonnaise 1 tbsp (15 mL) low-fat regular mayonnaise 1 tbsp (15 mL) regular salad dressing 2 tbsp (30 mL) light salad dressing
Sweets	1 tbsp (15 mL) maple syrup 1 tbsp (15 mL) sugar 1 tbsp (15 mL) jam or jelly ½ cup (125 mL) sherbet ½ cup (125 mL) low-fat or non-fat frozen yogurt

INCREASING POTASSIUM IN YOUR DIET

The DASH study showed that potassium in the foods we consume has a direct role in lowering blood pressure. In 2000 the US Food and Drug Administration recommended a diet high in potassium as a way to reduce the risk of high blood pressure and stroke.

Foods rich in potassium include fruits, fruit juices, vegetables, whole grains, dairy products and meat. Not all fruits and vegetables have the same amount of potassium, as you can see from these lists.

High Potassium Foods	Weight	Potassium content (mg)
Avocado	6 oz (180 g)	1097
V-8 juice, low sodium	1 cup (250 mL)	850
Baked potato with skin	7 oz (200 g)	820
Baked sweet potato	1 cup (250 mL)	774
Prunes, stewed	1 cup (250 mL)	774
Prune juice	1 cup (250 mL)	707
Kiwi fruit	1 cup (250 mL)	552
Orange juice	1 cup (250 mL)	524
Yogurt, low-fat vanilla	1 cup (250 mL)	498
Cantaloupe, honeydew	1 cup (250 mL)	494
Lima beans	½ cup (125 mL)	484
Banana	1 medium	454
Winter squash, baked	½ cup (125 mL)	448
Milk	1 cup (250 mL)	429
Spinach, cooked	½ cup (125 mL)	419
Tomatoes	1 cup (250 mL)	400
Corn	1 large ear	386
Lentils, cooked	½ cup (125 mL)	365
Papaya	1 cup (250 mL)	360
Molasses	1 tbsp (15 mL)	293
Apple	1 large	246
All meats, fish and poultry	½ cup (125 mL)	225

Moderate Potassium Foods
(125 to 225 mg per ½ cup, 125 mL serving)

Asparagus	Grapefruit
Beets	Green peas
Beans, yellow and green, fresh	Leaf lettuce
Bean sprouts	Mushrooms
Blackberries	Onions
Broccoli	Peaches
Carrots	Pears
Cauliflower	Pineapple
Cherries	

REDUCING SALT IN YOUR DIET

Reducing salt consumption by half would eliminate hypertension in one million Canadians and save the health-care system $430 million a year. These were the conclusions of a study published in the *Canadian Journal of Cardiology* in May 2007. Canadians are consuming excessive sodium, especially in the form of hidden salt in processed foods, and this causes high blood pressure leading to strokes and coronary heart disease.

The DASH diet containing 1500 mg of sodium (equivalent to about two-thirds of a teaspoon of table salt) per day has been found to be the most effective dietary way to reduce blood pressure. To achieve this level read the nutrition labels and choose food products that are labelled "low-sodium" or "sodium-free."

Here are some more ways to reduce sodium in your diet but still have tasty food.
- Use herbs and spices in cooking instead of salt.
- Make your own seasoning mix: combine garlic powder, onion powder, black pepper, oregano and basil.
- Season food with fresh lemon juice, lime juice or salt-free seasoning blends at the table.
- Buy fresh or frozen vegetables instead of canned ones that have salt added.
- Avoid fresh meat labelled "seasoned," which means it has been soaked in brine.
- Use fresh poultry, fish and lean meat rather than processed or canned products.
- Use whole-wheat pasta and brown rice, cooking them without salt.
- Cook vegetables without salt and experience their true flavour.
- Avoid or reduce consumption of monosodium glutamate, sodium citrate, baking soda, baking powder and sodium bicarbonate.
- Avoid sports drinks such as Gatorade, which are high in salt. Drink skimmed milk or water instead.

Sodium Content of Common Foods	Sodium (mg)
Table salt, 1 tsp (5 mL)	2300
Tomato sauce, canned, 1 cup (250 mL)	1482
Fish sauce, 1tbsp (15 mL)	1390
Chicken noodle soup, canned, 1 cup (250 mL)	1106
Baking Soda, 1 tsp (5 mL)	1080
Pretzels, 10	966
Soy sauce, 1 tbsp (15 mL)	938
Dill pickle, 1	928
Cottage cheese, 1 cup (250 mL)	911
Canned ham, 3 oz (90 g)	908
Chocolate pudding, 1 cup (250 mL)	880
English muffin, whole	378
Dijon mustard, 1 tbsp (15 mL)	370
Baking powder, 1 tsp (5 mL)	360
Shinho Highly Delicious Soy Sauce, 1 tbsp (15 ml)	145

Sodium Content of Popular Fast Foods	Sodium (mg)
McDonald's	
McDonald's quarter pounder with cheese	1110
Turkey BLT sandwich	1100
Burger King	
Enormous omelette sandwich	2000
Original whopper sandwich with cheese	1330
Wendy's	
Southwest chicken Caesar salad	1730
Premium fish fillet sandwich	1020
Dairy Queen	
DQ original bacon double cheeseburger	1550
Oreo cookie blizzard, large	770
Tim Horton's	
Turkey bacon club sandwich	1730
Chili	1320
Pizza Hut	
P'zone (Calzone)	1730
Chicken Alfredo	1300

What does salt-free mean?
140 mg sodium per serving is considered low-sodium; 35 mg or less per serving is considered very low-sodium; and 5 mg sodium is considered sodium-free.

Integrating recipes into the DASH eating plan

Here's a sample of a daily menu based on the recommendations of DASH that includes five recipes from this book. The number and category of servings is shown for each menu item. For example, ¾ cup (175 mL) orange juice equals 1 serving of fruit. The total number of servings is shown at the bottom of the menu as well as total nutrients for the day. This menu provides about 1800 calories, less than 1300 mg sodium and about 4700 mg potassium in accordance with DASH.

NO. OF SERVINGS FROM DASH FOOD GROUPS:

Grains 7	Meat 4
Vegetables 6	Nuts & Legumes 4.3
Fruits 5.5	Sweet 1.5
Dairy 6.25	Fat 1

DAILY NUTRIENT ANALYSIS:

Calories 1820	Sodium 1259mg
Calories from Fat 320 (18%)	Potassium 4706mg
Total Fat 37g	Carbohydrates 322g
Saturated Fat 6g	Fibre 38g
Cholesterol 54mg	Protein 70g

Sample Menu	# servings
Breakfast	
¾ cup (175 mL) orange juice	1 fruit
¾ cup (175 mL) bran flakes	1 grain
½ cup (125 mL) blueberries	1 fruit
1 cup (250 mL) non-fat milk	1 dairy
½ multigrain bagel	1 grain
1 ½ tsp jam	.5 sweet
Morning Snack	
1 oz (30 g) dried apricots	1 fruit
Lunch	
1 serving Japanese Style Salmon and Edamame Salad*	2 veg, .25 dairy, 2 meat, 1 fat,
1 oz (30 g) carrot sticks	1 veg
2 slices whole grain bread	2 grain
1 serving Creamy Rice Pudding*	.25 grain, .5 dairy, .5 sweet
Afternoon Snack	
1 banana	1 fruit
Dinner	
Chilled Zucchini Soup with Garlic Croutons and Dill*	3 grain, 1 veg, .3 dairy, .3 fat,
4 low-salt whole-wheat crackers	1 grain
Chicken and Artichoke Pasta with Almonds*	2 grains, 1 veg, 2 meat, .2 nuts
Green Beans	1 veg
Baked Apple with Dates and Nuts*	1.5 fruit, .1 nuts, .5 sweet

* Recipes in this book

DASH DINNER RECIPE GUIDE

All recipes in this book have reduced salt and can be incorporated into the DASH eating plan. To help you make choices, the following lists provide a sample of recipes with different sodium and potassium levels.

SODIUM-FREE less than 5 mg per serving

Steamed White or Brown Rice
Cool Cucumber & Red Onion Salad with Honey and Dill
Radicchio and Endive Salad with Maple Peach Dressing
Peach and Pepper Salsa
Apricot and Currant Chutney
Rhubarb Chutney
Peppered Strawberries with Balsamic Vinegar and Mint
Baked Apples with Dates and Nuts
Old-Fashioned Applesauce
Gingered Fruit Compote
Rum-Glazed Pineapple with Blueberries

VERY LOW SODIUM less than 35 mg per serving

Chicken Curry with Apricots and Almonds
Carolyn's Mediterranean Pasta Salad
Lentil, Wild Rice and Orzo Salad
Kushari
Spicy East Indian Cabbage
Four-Grain Pilaf with Currants and Cranberries
Linda's Watermelon Salad with Fresh Basil and Feta Cheese
Tangy Rainbow Slaw
Apricot Mousse with Grand Marnier

LOW SODIUM less than 140 mg per serving

Sicilian Chicken
Chicken and Artichoke Pasta with Almonds
Chinese Beef and Tomato with Peppers and Onions
Slow-Cooked Roast Beef with Wine Gravy
Roast Pork with Prune and Apple
Molasses-and-Rum-Glazed Salmon
Cornmeal-Crusted Salmon Cakes
Cajun Spiced Salmon with Tomato Salsa and Roasted Seaweed
Sesame-Halibut Kebabs with Pineapple and Honey
Madras Vegetable Curry
Spicy Dahl

HIGH POTASSIUM more than 600 mg per serving

*Barbecued Beef Sirloin and Black Bean Burgers
*Dan Hatfield's Beef and Beer Oven Stew
*Beef Tenderloin with Stilton on Mixed Greens
*Halibut with Mushrooms, Tomatoes and Artichokes
*Warm Scallop and Portobello Mushroom Salad
*Grilled Vegetable and Herbed Ricotta Napoleon
Sea Scallops with Wine and Lemon on Skewers
Spinach Sunshine Salad
Kieran's and Cam's Smashed Potatoes
Muskoka Fish Chowder

*contains more than 1000 mg potassium

GETTING A GRIP ON PORTION SIZE

A key to success in the DASH eating plan is understanding portion size. In an article in *Canadian Living* about DASH, Dr. Ernesto Schriffrin at the Clinical Research Institute of Montreal cautions his patients about large portion sizes, one of the causes of obesity, which in turn causes people to develop high blood pressure.

Most people don't understand what a serving is as they can't be bothered measuring out portions. When eating out, it is especially important to be wary as restaurant portions have become gigantic and often a plate of food is large enough to feed two people. In order not to overeat, my husband and I frequently order one appetizer, one salad and one entrée and share them. Another strategy to prevent overeating is to have part of your meal wrapped to take home for lunch the next day.

When you are serving food at home, keep the following guidelines in mind.

- 1 Pasta or Rice serving equals ½ cup (125 mL), about the amount you could hold in the cupped palm of your hand.
- 1 Fruit or Vegetable serving cooked equals ½ cup (125 mL) cooked, the amount you could hold in the cupped palm of your hand.
- 1 Cheese serving equals 1 ½ oz (45 g), a piece the size of your thumb.
- 1 Milk or Yogurt serving equals 1 cup (250 mL), about the size of your fist.
- 1 Meat or Fish serving of 3oz (90 g) is a piece the size of a deck of playing cards.

DASH PUBLICATIONS

My favourite resources are the NIH website and *The DASH Diet for Hypertension* written by the DASH study researchers. They explain the research behind DASH and provide suggestions for following the diet as well as menus and recipes. The Heart and Stroke Foundation of Canada and Mayo Clinic Web sites provide helpful information on DASH as well.

National Institutes of Health, National Heart, Lung, and Blood Institute. *Your Guide To Lowering Your Blood Pressure With DASH*. NIH Publication No. 06-4082. Originally Printed 1998. Revised April 2006. www.nih.gov Search DASH.

Moore, T., L. Svetkey., P-H. Lin, N. Karanja with M. Jenkins. *The DASH Diet for Hypertension*. New York: Pocket Books (Simon & Schuster), 2003.

Heart and Stroke Foundation of Canada. *The DASH Diet to Lower High Blood Pressure*. www.heartandstroke.com Search DASH.

Mayo Clinic. *DASH Diet*. www.mayoclinic.com Search DASH.

INDEX